FRONTIER LAW

ALSO FROM WESTPHALIA PRESS
WESTPHALIAPRESS.ORG

FRONTIER LAW

<><><><><><><><><><>

A STORY OF VIGILANTE DAYS

BY WILLIAM J. MCCONNELL

WESTPHALIA PRESS
An imprint of Policy Studies Organization

Westphalia Press
An imprint of Policy Studies Organization
1527 New Hampshire Ave., NW
Washington, D.C. 20036
info@ipsonet.org

ISBN-13: 978-1-63391-257-1
ISBN-10: 1633912574

Cover design by Taillefer Long at Illuminated Stories:
www.illuminatedstories.com

Daniel Gutierrez-Sandoval, Executive Director
PSO and Westphalia Press

Updated material and comments on this edition
can be found at the Westphalia Press website:
www.westphaliapress.org

Frontier Law

"Stepping inside and immediately facing my audience, I exclaimed, 'Well! Show your colors.'" (See page 143.)

Pioneer Life Series

FRONTIER LAW

A Story of Vigilante Days

By William J. McConnell

In collaboration with
Howard R. Driggs
New York University

With an Introduction by
Senator William E. Borah

Illustrated with drawings by
Herbert M. Stoops

WORLD BOOK COMPANY

THE HOUSE OF APPLIED KNOWLEDGE

Established 1905 by Caspar W. Hodgson

YONKERS-ON-HUDSON, NEW YORK
2126 PRAIRIE AVENUE, CHICAGO

Gold and blood, Indians and pioneers, bad men and Vigilantes! These are terms that have captivated the imagination of young America for generations. Nevertheless, authentic, first-hand accounts of the Vigilantes have been few indeed. The reason is plain : no man who helped to dispense the rough and salutary justice of the frontier thought it discreet to tell what he knew. But after the passing of sixty years, when time has healed all wounds, William J. McConnell, once Governor of Idaho and also United States Senator, has come forth with a story that makes the blood leap. In matter-of-fact fashion, and as vividly as if he were relating events of the day before yesterday, he tells of the overland journey to the Coast, of placer mining in California shortly after the wild days of '49, of homesteading in Oregon, and of farming and prospecting in Idaho. Most unusual and interesting of all, he tells the inside story of the Vigilantes, who restored control of territorial affairs to the decent people of Idaho when bad men and their satellites in office had made a mockery of the processes of justice and government. World Book Company is gratified to be able to present to Americans of all ages, but particularly to young Americans, Governor McConnell's *Frontier Law*, a story of the triumph of sturdy manhood over natural and man-made obstacles in days when the West was wild

Δ

PLS : MCCFL- 2

AN INTRODUCTION TO THE AUTHOR

BORN in the frontier woodlands of old Michigan; trained to hunt and to shoot by an Indian boy friend, who was a direct descendant of the famous Chief Pontiac; led by a spirit of adventure into the wildest parts of the far West, there to become captain of a band of Vigilantes, and to lend a firm hand in bringing law and order into a region where red-handed lawlessness held sway — this in a word is the story of the earlier life of the author of this book. He tells that story here in straightforward style with convincing human touches.

It is another romance of reality, with illuminating side-lights on our country's great story, that is brought to us in this little volume. In the opening chapters the pioneer days in the Grand River Valley of the Wolverine State are made to live again; then we are taken westward across the plains by mule train. The old placer "diggin's" in California, after the thrilling days of the gold rush of '49 had gone by, are clearly pictured; Oregon likewise, while the sturdy pioneers were yet carving out their homesteads from the virgin forests, is brought realistically before us. Then come stirring stories of the new gold rush for the Boisé Basin, with its tragic outlawry, and finally the rising of the long-suffering citizenry who gradually grip the situation and establish orderly government with consequent peace and prosperity.

A clear note of Americanism rings through every part of the story. Love of liberty, respect for law, a desire for learning, reverence for God — all are blended in this life story of a real American boy, of good old Scotch parentage. Industry, sobriety, and virtue, coupled with a willingness to face squarely the issues of life, and to fight ever for the right, are the vital lessons that are echoed from its every chapter.

With these fundamentals of success woven into his

character by loving parents, it is small wonder that William J. McConnell should have so risen in the esteem of the people in his adopted state of Idaho as to be chosen one of its first United States senators, and later to be elected as governor of the same great commonwealth. Nor is it to be wondered that even now, at the ripe age of more than fourscore years, he should still be firm of step, and clear of mind, carrying forward his life of service.

It was my good fortune to meet this keen-eyed, up-standing veteran some years ago in his home city of Moscow, Idaho. Eager as always for first-hand stories of our pioneers, I was soon listening to Governor McConnell while he told some of those stories he still held in vivid memory. Then nothing would satisfy but a promise on his part to write for the youth of America and for the world a few at least of those stirring experiences of his earlier life. With characteristic promptness, he had soon fulfilled that promise.

The book has been long delayed in the publishing, however, largely because of an earnest search to find the artist who best could bring out with clear, sure strokes the inner spirit of the story. At last one was found whose earlier life had been spent in old Idaho. That this artist from the far West has done his work with rare skill and true joy is manifest in every sketch he has given to help illuminate and interpret the heart of the theme.

And now we send this little volume forth with the hope that it will help to cultivate in the Boy Scouts, to whom the author desires this book especially to be dedicated, and to all other boys and girls as well as the older folk, a deeper love for our country, and an abiding respect for the laws of our land. Only in such a love and such a respect can we ever be secure in the liberties we cherish.

HOWARD R. DRIGGS

CONTENTS

vii

OUR AMERICAN PIONEERS

THIS volume records the observations and experiences of one of the most interesting and remarkable figures of pioneer days in the Far West. Of unusual intellect, tireless energy, superb courage, he saw and experienced pioneer life in all its manifold and dramatic phases. And now, more than fifty years afterward, with precision and accuracy, he gives his observations and experiences to the printed page. The book will prove interesting, not only to those who love the West and who have chanced to know some of these sturdy men now rapidly passing off the stage, but interesting and instructive also to the students of national growth and development — to those who love to dwell upon the great achievements in our national history. There is no part of our history more tense with human interest, richer, or more thrilling in instances of individual daring and superb personal courage, than may be found in the story of the opening and development of the Far West. It is to be hoped that this volume may lead others of the pioneer days to recount their experiences — too much of such history we can scarcely have.

It has been my privilege to listen to many of these pioneers recount their experiences and in homely phrase and graphic fashion recall scenes which are in many respects without precedent or parallel. It is a story which never grows old. The elements of character which all must admire are never wanting. Self-reliance, a grim and purposeful outlook on life, willingness to risk, resourcefulness in hours of great peril, and through it all a fine strain of Americanism, loyalty to the fundamental principles of free government, make the story of the pioneer one of absorbing interest and, moreover, one of inspiration.

Invading a wilderness, a region without order, a vast country without law, traveling strange paths and adopting sometimes harsh and startling methods, nevertheless, the ultimate aim was great commonwealths, a country dedicated to orderly and regulated liberty. The pioneer was not merely an adventurer seeking gold, he was an empire builder; he laid a broad and firm foundation for these great commonwealths. They are in the true sense the real monuments to the pioneer.

Reference to the pioneer, however brief, would be both incomplete and unfair without special mention of the pioneer woman. Justice cannot be rendered in an introductory article, but at least mention must be made. What a marvel of patience, of devotion, of indefinable charm and tenderness, even amid the roughest environments of the desert; and above all, what self-control and courage in the hour of imminent peril! Some gifted pen will sometime, I trust, pay a fitting tribute to this sublime exhibition of American womanhood.

The story of the pioneer is rapidly passing beyond our control. It lies almost exclusively in the memory of the actors. But few of these are left. Some of them still pass among us, honored and revered by all. We realize fully the sacrifices they made, the hardships endured, that we who followed might enjoy wholesome and prosperous communities and live under the shelter of great states. The story of their lives, the history of their times, should be preserved to the fullest extent possible. I wish we were able to preserve more of this great epic in our national life.

WILLIAM E. BORAH

"Young Pontiac and I soon became intimate friends."

CHAPTER ONE

BOYHOOD DAYS IN OLD MICHIGAN

MY parents were born in Ireland, of Scotch ancestry. Soon after their marriage they emigrated to New York, where they joined a company of like nationality and journeyed on into Michigan. At this time and for many years thereafter, this state was regarded as being in the Far West. It was here on the frontier in the "Wolverine State" that I was born in 1839. The Indians at that time in Michigan were an uncertain element, and caused much uneasiness to the pioneers, but fortunately there was no Indian outbreak after the arrival of my parents and their company.

When I was fourteen years of age, my parents moved still farther into the wilds, this time settling in the Grand River Valley, Ionia County. Our new home was located only three miles above a Pottawatamie Indian village, which occupied a bend of the Grand River. Upon our arrival a party of these Indians was making maple sugar in the woods less than half a mile from where our log house was built. We were greatly interested in watching them.

Among the party of Indians was a lad one or two years older than I. He was a direct descendant of the famous Chief Pontiac; and he was named Pontiac, after his proud ancestor. Since this boy of royal Indian blood was not required to do any work around the sugar camp, he spent his time hunting and trapping.

Young Pontiac and I soon became intimate friends. From that friendship my opportunity came to acquire a knowledge of woodcraft. I also gained from him skill in trailing both men and animals, which has often served me well since entering the wilds west of the Mississippi River.

Grand River Valley was then but sparsely settled. The pioneers who had ventured into and undertaken to carve homes from the beech and maple forest might have been classed as hunters rather than farmers. Most of them had but a few acres cleared and under cultivation, and such clearings were thickly studded with stumps. The sons of these settlers at an early age were required to perform nearly the work of a grown man. They became expert in the use of an ax, as clearing off their land by chopping down the trees and burning them was their principal employment. Hunting and trapping wild animals was their chief recreation, so the use of a rifle was as familiar to these pioneer boys as was the use of an ax.

The first work of the settlers was to erect houses of unhewn logs in which to shelter their families. There were no sawmills available, so lumber for doors and floors was whipsawed by hand. The second year a schoolhouse was erected, designed to serve also as a church.

In that crude building I was taught, first the mysteries of a Webster Spelling Book, including columns of abbreviations, and later to "cipher." The schoolhouse was built of logs. Upon the ceiling-joists of smaller logs was laid a covering of split clapboards, which lacked uniformity in width and thickness and did not lie closely together. As a consequence there were many cracks which served as ventilators. The roof also was covered with the same kind of clapboards. Nails were scarce, and the smallest number possible were used. Clapboards such as these, riven out of oak, when exposed to the sun have a tendency to warp if not securely nailed in place, so the corners and sometimes the sides of the boards turned up; and when the winter storms broke upon us the drifting snow penetrated every opening and lodged upon the ceiling. It was melted by the heat from the fire below, and dripped down upon the pupils.

The trustees called a meeting to devise a way to keep the pupils from taking an involuntary shower bath. They decided to try spreading dry oak leaves upon the ceiling and covering them with a few inches of sand, hoping that the sand would absorb the water from the melting snow and stop the leaking. This plan was carried out. The covering of leaves was spread over the ceiling, and sand spread over the leaves to a depth of several inches. The sand being moist as it came out of the pit, served well at first. But alas for the ingenuity of our fathers; the heat from below soon dried the sand until it too would run like water. Then, as sometimes happened, when a chipmunk or mouse ran over the sand, a little stream of it would start for the schoolroom below, frequently striking the boys or girls on the backs of their necks as they bent over their books. The next thing the startled pupils knew the insinuating sand was covering their feet.

There were never enough books to go around. Two
boys or girls, sitting side by side, often studied their
lesson out of the same book. We would stand in line to
read, the exercise beginning at the head of the class and
the book being passed down the line until it reached the
next fortunate pupil who possessed one.

One afternoon while our school was in session, during
the early winter months, a team of horses hitched to a
light spring wagon halted at the front of our schoolhouse.
The driver came to the door and called to our teacher.
After a short conversation they both came into the schoolroom, and our teacher told us that the stranger was a book
agent who wanted to introduce a new series of schoolbooks,
published in Boston, and that, as an inducement to us
to adopt his series, he was willing to exchange new books
for our old ones, book for book.   The agent assured us that
he would supply the store at our local village, three miles
distant, with sufficient books to meet the demands of all
the schools in the township.   Our teacher advised us to
accept the proposition; so within a few minutes all our
old thumb-worn books were transferred to his wagon, and
the new volumes lay on our desks.

The next summer, while hunting rabbits in a thicket of
huckleberry bushes located in the midst of a swamp, I
came upon our old schoolbooks, together with many more,
for which the agent had exchanged new books at schools
he had visited.   With the curiosity of a boy I proceeded to
investigate my find, and turning over book after book, I
found that most of them were badly damaged by exposure.
But underneath the pile I found a leather-covered volume
which proved to be a Kirkham's Grammar, practically
uninjured.   The book agent evidently had dumped the
old exchange books he had received where he supposed
they would never be discovered.

Printed as a kind of preface to the grammar was an address to the students, extolling our land as a "land of liberty." This "boon of freedom," the address continued, had been "purchased by the blood of our forefathers." It urged further that "upon the intelligence of our youth depend the future glory and grandeur of our beloved country," and closed with the exhortation, "Become learned and virtuous and you will become great; love God and you will be happy."

It being customary in our school to require pupils to "speak a piece" at certain fixed intervals, I committed to memory that address and it became an inspiration to me during my subsequent struggle to gain an education. Later I learned that one of the few books possessed by Abraham Lincoln, when he was a boy, was a Kirkham's Grammar; and that he memorized that same address, while lying before an open fireplace in his log-cabin home. I have no doubt that its stirring and patriotic sentiments helped to rouse patriotism and stimulate ambition for learning in that backwoods boy, upon whom in subsequent years devolved such great responsibility.

With the exception of one boy of uncertain age, all of the pupils in our school were well-behaved and studious. This boy, in consequence of disobedience and violation of the rules of the school, was often disciplined. After being punished, as soon as he was out of the teacher's hearing, he would use terrible oaths, and declare that as soon as he was big enough he would "lick that teacher." As a natural consequence of his lawless actions, the boy was finally expelled from school. Soon afterwards he was convicted of theft and sent to the state reform school.

It is not pleasant to relate such incidents of failure or of lost opportunity. My only thought in doing so is to bring to the notice of my young friends the importance of obedience to law. The wishes of a father or mother are the elementary laws of every household. The boy who disobeys his parents is likely to violate the rules at school. And the rules governing a school are rudimentary forms of law, which are but stepping stones to the higher forms. Violations of law bring not only punishment but disgrace and broken hearts.

It is earnestly hoped that the youth of America will use their influence to help one another obey the laws of their city, their county, their state, and their country. It is expected that the teacher will make it a prime duty always to instill in the minds of boys and girls a respect for the laws of the land. On intelligent obedience to law our liberties depend.

The American pioneers, realizing the importance of this training, have ever been ready to sacrifice some of their meager means to establish schools that would help the parents in their efforts to give their children the proper start in life. Although Grand River Valley was but sparsely settled when our family moved into it, each community had its district school, and a teacher was employed at least six months each year. During this time my parents kept me continually in attendance.

We had little ready money with which to pay the teacher. Cash was a scarce article in Grand River Valley in those days. There was only one method of obtaining actual money to pay taxes and to meet such expenses as require cash payment. This was the making and selling of lye. First we gathered ashes from the spot where we burned the logs in clearing the land. These ashes were leached by passing water through them. The lye thus obtained was boiled down in large iron kettles until it became what was called by the pioneers "black salts," now known as concentrated lye.

In disposing of the lye, it was customary for a party of two or more neighbors to unite in making a trip to the nearest market, more than one hundred miles distant. Each would furnish in turn a yoke of oxen to haul the wagon used to carry the "black salts." Generally a few furs also were taken to exchange for such necessaries as are indispensable in a frontier home. The "black salts" were readily sold for actual cash to meet the annual visit of the tax collector, and the rate bill levied to pay the school-teacher.

At the age of eighteen, I took the necessary examination to obtain a teacher's certificate. During the three following winters I taught a district school for a term of three months, to earn enough to pursue my studies during the rest of the year. When not engaged in teaching or attending school I helped my father chop a farm out of the beech and maple forest. After my twentieth birthday, feeling keenly the loss of my mother, who had died the previous autumn, I started on my journey in search of adventure in the farther West.

"A Pony Express rider came dashing up behind us and went racing and whooping past our train."

CHAPTER TWO

THE UPS AND DOWNS OF MULE DRIVING

LEAVENWORTH, Kansas, was the frontier town from which I took my plunge into the wilds of the plains and the mountains. I learned there that a firm named Perry Brothers, with headquarters at Weston, Missouri, was outfitting a freight train of sixteen freight wagons, to be drawn each by six mules, and that this train was to deliver merchandise at Salt Lake City, Utah. Drivers were being hired for the journey. I immediately decided that I would try to secure a job with that outfit. That night I suffered from a severe bilious attack, so I should not have undertaken the journey to Weston the next morning; but eager to get a position as driver, and fearful that if I delayed the places would all be taken, I took the chance. Crossing the Missouri River on a ferry-boat, I started up the river bottom on foot.

At that time, April, 1860, there was no clearing opposite Leavenworth City. The woods extended down to high-water mark. I soon discovered that my illness of the previous night had left me too weak for the journey I had planned. After plodding along as best I could through dense woods along a road which apparently was seldom traveled, I eventually arrived at a clearing in which was a double log house with an outside stick chimney at each end. There was smoke issuing from one of the chimneys.

I approached the door and rapped "Come in," was the response. Upon pulling the proverbial "latch string" and stepping inside, I found myself in a large room. Its sole occupant was a motherly appearing old lady, who occupied a rocking chair by the fireplace and was engaged at knitting when disturbed by my knock. A glance revealed that the room contained two double beds, besides a kitchen table and sundry other pieces of household furniture.

I informed the old lady that I was on my way to Weston, but had been taken ill and was unable to continue on my journey that day, and that I wished to remain with them until I was able to travel. I said I would pay for my entertainment.

"Why you have a fever," she exclaimed; "undress and get right into this bed." She at once proceeded to spread down the covers.

I hesitated to undress, but finally I partly disrobed and was tucked in as tenderly as could have been done by my own mother. The good woman then proceeded to make me a hot drink, steeping herbs which were hanging in little bundles above the mantel. This she required me to take at intervals.

It was Friday morning when I entered that hospitable home, and the following Monday I was able to proceed. I accordingly asked my hostess how much I owed for my entertainment, and she replied that board was $1.50 per week, and as I had been there since Friday, we would call it half a week, — say "six bits." I insisted that was not sufficient to pay her for her care and trouble, but she declared it was no trouble.

Before I started on my way the old man of the place took me out and showed me his clearing. He told me that he " 'lowed to plant a right smart chance of corn that year." I have ever carried with me the memory of that sample of good old Missouri hospitality.

Before noon that day I arrived at Weston. Learning that the office of Perry Brothers was located at a flouring mill which they operated, a short distance from the business section of the city, I went there at once. Upon my arrival, before entering the office, I met a young man of rough exterior who asked me if I wanted to hire to drive mules to Salt Lake.

"Yes," I replied.

"Good," he responded; "I have just hired for the trip, and we will be partners."

Upon entering the office I was engaged at once, and told to come back the next morning for instructions. Returning to the street I found my new acquaintance waiting for me. He informed me that he had found a restaurant kept by a German who gave his boarders plenty of eggs and other good things to eat at a very reasonable price. We were entertained there the remainder of that day and the following night.

The next morning we were instructed to go to a certain ranch several miles southwest from Atchison, Kansas. There we were to assist the men who were already at the ranch in caring for a band of 120 mules which were to furnish the motive power to haul the freight wagons across the plains to Salt Lake City.

Not being provided with animals to ride, we had to walk, and the distance proved long and tiresome. It was late in the afternoon when we reached Atchison.

Waiting only long enough to obtain explicit directions as to the road to the ranch, we started immediately to cover the distance — seven more long miles. Darkness dropped down upon us before we had gone more than half the way. Being hungry and exhausted after a long weary tramp, my friend proposed that we turn in at a haystack and remain until morning. He was more experienced in camp life than I, but although we each were carrying a pair of blankets and could have kept comfortably warm I refused to accept his suggestion, stating that some person might see us in the morning before we had departed and take us for horse thieves. We therefore plodded on and eventually arrived at the camp where the mules were being held.

This camp was simply an open-air bivouac, in a yard where was stored a lot of corn fodder. We did not arrive until the three men in charge were in bed. Their beds consisted of blankets spread in the open. One of them did the cooking; but we were too late for supper. In fact, I was so tired that I did not feel like eating, and soon we too were wrapped in our blankets with the blinking stars our only canopy.

That night I gained my first knowledge of the life of an early-day mule driver. For one thing they did not, before lying down, remove their outer clothing; perhaps they had acquired this habit because many of them had no undergarments. Almost my entire life until that time had been passed on the frontier, both white men and Indians being my companions, yet I had had generally a roof above me at night, and a bed spread by a mother's loving hands, with fluffy feather pillows under my head. This was a sudden transition to a different kind of frontier life.

Later I learned by experience to judge the quality or weight of blankets. In purchasing a pair for a covering while crossing the continent I do not recollect that I examined them as to either weight or texture; they were a dark blue and looked good to me; I asked the price, and paid it, — $3.50.   On that first night at the mule camp early in April I was brought to a shivering realization that there might be a difference in the warmth of blankets.

We were aroused before sunrise the following morning by the braying of the mules.   Our first task was to carry out and distribute a quantity of corn and corn fodder. After this we were called to breakfast, which consisted of fat fried bacon, hot rolls, and black coffee.

To water the mules it was necessary to drive them twice each day to a little creek two or three miles distant.   The foreman at the camp designated the men who were to take the mules to water.   It required two men to handle them, one riding ahead of the band, the other behind to urge on any stragglers which might drop out of the herd.

The first step was to catch from the herd two animals for the men to ride; this was accomplished by casting a lariat over the necks of the animals.   Sometimes in the confusion caused by the mules continually moving about, the lariat would fall upon different mules from the ones selected, but the man who had made the cast would not admit his error, lest the others ridicule him; consequently he might have a mount which had never been even haltered before.   The man who was to ride ahead and lead the herd would wait at the corral gate, which at a given signal was thrown open.   At the same instant the other man who had succeeded in cinching a saddle on the obstreperous mule vaulted up and dashed out through the gate after the band, his mule bucking and bawling.   But unwilling to be left behind the other mules, it would buck or pitch straight ahead, thus making it easier for its rider to keep his seat.

It soon became known for a distance of several miles that there was a "free circus" at that mule camp twice a day. The result was that there were usually a dozen or more spectators. My friend Pontiac had instructed me in the art of throwing the lariat, and the lessons he had given me made it easy to catch any mule I wished to ride. As I was required to do my regular turn at driving the mules to water, I soon was able to ride fairly well, but I never recovered from a wholesome dread of the heels of a mule.

A few days after my arrival at camp we received a big load of harness, "knocked down"; that is, the parts had not been put together. We were at once set at work assembling them. There were enough for ninety-six mules, or forty-eight sets of heavy double harness. The intent of the owners, as already said, was to fit out and load sixteen freight wagons. Each wagon was to be drawn by six mules, and was to be driven by a single line. The drivers each rode the near-wheel mule.

As soon as the harness was assembled, it was reloaded into the wagon which brought it out, and mules and men were started for Atchison, where, we were informed, our wagons and freight had arrived. Upon our arrival there, we found that the other drivers who had been employed were already there, and had most of the wagons loaded. We soon learned that it was the intention of the owners to make forced drives and reach Salt Lake City as early as possible, consequently the wagons were to be loaded light, only 3000 pounds, or one and one-half tons, each, which was a light load for six mules.

The animals were immediately corralled, and then began the sport of catching each mule and fitting on the harness. This operation quickly revealed that but few of the mules had ever been broken to harness. We learned that in purchasing the mules the owners endeavored to provide enough broken animals so that each team of six mules might be provided with two which were broken, the near lead mule and the driver's saddle mule. As rapidly as the mules were selected for each team and the harness fitted to them they were led out and tied to the wheels of the wagon they were to haul. When the selections were made, each driver was assigned to his wagon and team. The wagons were all provided with bows and double sheeting covers numbered from one to sixteen, inclusive.

We soon learned that we were to have a professional wagon boss, and in addition to him we were to be accompanied by one of the owners, a blacksmith, night-herder, and the driver who was to drive a light spring wagon in which the owner or any of his select party, the blacksmith, or wagon boss might ride when fatigued in the saddle. The driver of the mules which hauled the light spring wagon was also the steward and cook for his mess.

Atchison at the time of our departure, April 23, 1860, was a town of no great size. The harnessing of so many wild mules and starting out on such a journey as ours provided entertainment for most of the population — men, women, and children alike. However, we finally succeeded in hitching up the teams to their respective wagons, and with the wagon boss and blacksmith riding in front we started for Salt Lake City.

The first day we traveled but a few miles, and went into camp on the open prairie on the bank of a little stream ; here we unhitched and unharnessed our mules. Trail ropes had been provided to us, and before turning the mules loose, each driver attached one to the neck of every mule. Here the rope was to remain until the train reached its destination. At this first camp the drivers were divided into two messes of five each and one of six. The several duties of camp life were also apportioned, each man in turn performing his allotted task.

Before leaving Atchison I asked the wagon boss how many pairs of blankets I would need, and he told me that one pair would be plenty, as I could double up with one of the other drivers. Tenderfoot as I was I did not recognize the grim humor of starting across the plains in April with only one pair of blankets, but I had a better understanding of bedding after the first night out, when I discovered that no tents were provided in which to sleep. Upon inquiry we were told that we could sleep under the wagons. The shelter of the wagons was all right when we did not need shelter, during fair weather; but during stormy nights when the wind howled, and the rain fell in torrents, it does not require a very vivid imagination to picture the discomfort of a bed under a wagon. However, the drivers were all young men, and it seemed as if neither rain, snow, nor hail discouraged or affected them.

The drivers, in addition to harnessing and unharnessing their six mules — usually twice a day — were required to do their own cooking. Furthermore, they must stand guard one half the night every other night to prevent the mules from straying too far from camp or being stolen by Indians or white men.

During the first two weeks nothing occurred to relieve the monotony of our everyday routine. One afternoon, however, while we were approaching the Big Sandy in Nebraska, a Pony Express rider came dashing up behind us and went racing and whooping past our train. The sudden appearance of the horse and rider put our wild mules in a panic. First the hindmost team stampeded, then one after another followed until the entire outfit of sixteen wagons and an ambulance were being propelled across the prairie as rapidly as frightened mules could navigate.   After racing one another several hundred yards, some of the mules become weary, and began to slow down. Others did likewise, until the entire train finally came to a halt.   One of the drivers had suffered a broken arm during the stampede, and we were compelled to leave him at the Big Sandy, where he could receive the attendance of a surgeon.

The Pony Express had started out from St. Joe, Missouri, on its first trip across the continent, the same day our train left Atchison, Kansas, April 23, 1860.   Our stampede marked its first appearance on the route we were traveling.   The Pony Express was the precursor of the Overland Stage, the telegraph, and the railroad which followed a few years later.

Up to the inauguration of the Pony Express, it required an average of thirty days for a letter to reach San Francisco from New York.   The schedule time of the Pony Express was only ten days from St. Joe, Missouri, to Sacramento, California.   Regular express stations were established for the ponies and riders at intervals where water and other conveniences could be provided.   These were generally eight to ten miles apart.   Sometimes they were twenty to thirty, or even fifty.

When it happened that these stations were attacked by Indians, the keepers killed, and the station burned, the rider made a detour, circling the smoking ruins, or if no Indians were in sight, rushed past on to the next station. Their pace, a rapid gallop, was never broken, day or night, between stations.   Five dollars an ounce was the price for carrying letters.

Fortunately for the Pony Express men, as well as others on the plains that year, the Indians east of Salt Lake City were friendly.   They did not interfere with travelers, most of whom were not armed or equipped to resist attack.

As a sample, the train in which I was one of the drivers had only half a dozen discarded army Harper's Ferry Yagers, for which we had no fixed ammunition.

In recalling the defenseless condition in which our train made the journey from Atchison to Salt Lake City, it appears incredible that sane and experienced men would have risked their lives and such an amount of valuable property without making adequate provision for protection. Had the twenty-one men in our party been armed with such rifles as most of the men had been accustomed to use, no ordinary raiding party of Indians, armed as most of them were with bows and arrows, would have dared to attack us. Yet we escaped, but it was more by fool luck than good judgment. The Indians probably did not realize that we were so poorly armed and at their mercy.

It was apparently too early in the season for buffalo to be encountered on the Overland Trail, which we were following. We found no game except a few antelope. However, we devoted no time to hunting, but pushed steadily ahead day after day, without unnecessary delay, arriving at Salt Lake City, the first through wagon train of the season, fifty-three days after we started.

The drivers were paid off the following morning, at the agreed rate of one dollar per day, $53. Nearly all of them began to search for conveyance on to California. We learned upon our arrival that the Indians west of Salt Lake, recognized by the appropriate title of Gosiutes ("Go-shoots"), were on the warpath, and that in consequence the Pony Express service had been temporarily abandoned, as some of the stations had been burned and the horses had run off. The number of riders who had been killed was unknown, several days having elapsed since communication was cut off.

Upon our arrival at Salt Lake City we found a party

with a train of horses on the way to the California market. They were anxious to take as passengers three more men, each of whom might have two horses, one to ride and one to lead. When this became known to our men, there was a stampede to secure the opportunity. To settle the matter the owners left the choice to the wagon boss of our mule train. Fortunately or otherwise I was named as one of the three chosen ones; probably because I had demonstrated my skill with firearms.

"Their signal fires were flashing forth at intervals from every mountain."

CHAPTER THREE

BATTLING THROUGH THE DESERTS

SALT Lake City at the time of our advent, 1860, was an unpretentious city of domestic quietude. It was so totally at variance from towns on the Missouri River, with their riotous confusion, that I would have gladly remained a few days, rather than venture out again upon the terrors of the unknown deserts in the West; but the owners of the horses were anxious to get the stock out of the city, to a place where they could find grass. As soon as it was determined which of our drivers would be accepted, we started upon what was destined to be the most eventful part of our journey across the continent.

Even at that early day a few settlers had ventured west of Salt Lake City, and had located farms in little valleys, wherever water was available. We were told that probably the Indians would not be seen until after we had passed those settlements. This proved to be true. It was not until the following night, after we had passed the

19

last settlement, that we saw signs of Indians; — then their signal fires were flashing forth at intervals from every mountain in the direction we were traveling. Every indication tended to confirm the report that there was a general uprising of the Indians between the Salt Lake settlements and the newly discovered mineral fields adjacent to Carson Valley.

Practically all the intervening country through which we must pass was a treeless, alkaline desert. Water could be found only at long distances apart, and then only in limited quantity. To avoid the intense heat we adopted the custom of traveling at night, and remaining in camp during the day; but while night travel was easier for the horses, it gave the men less opportunity to sleep, for the reason that guards were necessary to prevent surprise. A strong guard was maintained not only near the camp, but with the horses, as they were usually herded some distance from camp, among the foothills, where the best grass was always found.

We passed several of the Pony Express stations, or rather the charred remains of what had been stations, before we saw a white person. Early one morning, before daybreak and after traveling all night, we came suddenly upon an oasis in the desert, in which we found an inclosure probably a hundred feet square, made by throwing up a wall of earth faced with sods. The wall was about four feet high, and within this inclosure were two wagons, the beds from which covered by bows and canvas had been removed and lowered to the ground where they were used as sleeping quarters by two men and their wives.

Our arrival aroused them. We were soon informed that the Pony Express was no longer an express, as every station from that place to the Slough of Carson had been burned. The express riders had either run off or been killed. That so many of them escaped with their lives was no doubt due to the fact that the Indians on those desert plains had no horses, and could not pursue and capture their intended victims. Once a rider gained the back of his horse he had a fairly good chance to escape; and one or more horses were kept continually saddled and ready for an emergency.

The oasis at which we had so opportunely arrived was in extent approximately a hundred acres, and under a cliff of rocks at the upper end a stream gushed out from a strong spring, only to sink and disappear a few hundred yards farther on. There were no trees, not even a willow bush, but the entire area was covered with grass, as if it had been planted by the hand of man. Our horses were sorely in need of rest, grass, and water. The men also, having had but little sleep or rest for ten days and nights, were in as poor physical condition as the horses. We were all young men, however, in the prime of life and health, consequently after we had been given a few hours sleep and a hearty meal, we were ready to take the trail again.

The two men and their wives whom we found at that oasis on the Utah desert were thorough plainsmen and plainswomen. They were employed by the Pony Express company to care for that station. When notice of the Indian outbreak came they had concluded that it was safer for them to remain within their inclosure than to attempt escape over the long distance to a settlement. They informed us that two nights previous to our arrival two agents of the Pony Express company had arrived at their inclosure and remained until morning, when they started on westward.

The Indians who had doubtless been watching the station day after day hoping for an opportunity to make an attack, saw two men riding away from the station, and seeing no one moving about the wagons, thought the men they saw were the station keepers, and that the women were left for a time alone. They waited until the travelers were over the ridge out of sight from the station, and then they started for their intended victims. A distance of three or four miles intervened between the dividing ridge, where the Indians were concealed and waiting, and the station. It required some time even for an Indian to cover that distance.

The men and women of the station, who were no less alert than the Indians, had discovered their approach. Keeping quiet they permitted the redskins to advance. There were three Indians approaching. The station keepers did not announce their presence until the Indians approached the gate to the inclosure. Then jumping out of the wagon beds, they opened fire at the savages, but as the Indians were running and dodging, the shots were without effect. Horses were saddled, mounted, and pursuit began. Both pursuers were armed with Colt's navy revolvers, while the Indians were provided with only bows and arrows. The result of the pursuit was as anticipated by the wives: the fleeing Indians were overtaken halfway to the hills, where they hoped to obtain refuge, and killed.

We remained two days at this delightful little oasis, and the second night, with horses and men refreshed, we continued our journey westward. From that point until we arrived at the Slough of Carson our progress was interrupted at several places where Indians were concealed in rocky cañons through which we were compelled to pass. In all these encounters the Indians' fire appeared to be directed at our horses more than at the men. They evidently ate the horses and were hungry for fresh meat.

The outlet to Carson Lake, which we had learned was called the "Slough" or "Sink" of Carson, we found to be a swiftly running, deep stream. As there was no ferry boat and it barred our further progress, some method of crossing the wagons, men, and supplies must be devised; the horses we could cross by swimming them. There were two logs on the opposite bank, approximately fourteen feet long and about twelve inches in diameter. These would serve the purpose of a raft if roped together with a wagon box fastened on top, provided we could manage to float them across to our side. Inquiry was made to ascertain which of our party could swim. Being questioned, I answered in the affirmative, and accordingly, with another young man, I was directed to strip and cross for the logs. We swam the slough without difficulty, carrying with us one end of a rope, which our men on the bank paid out as we progressed. Arriving at the logs, we rolled them into the water and fastened the line to them and started back. Resting our arms on the logs, we were towed across, where we soon dressed in a hurry to escape the mosquitoes, which delighted in our nakedness.

One of our wagons had been unloaded and the bed removed while we were crossing the logs. The primitive raft, by means of which we could transfer our goods and chattels, was quickly made. The horses were made to swim without difficulty, a feat which is not always possible, for the reason that some horses cannot swim. Before darkness fell that evening we had safely transferred all our belongings and our horses.

Being within less than twenty miles from the new Eldorado, Virginia City, we imagined that we were safe from further attack by Indians. We were beyond the reach of the "Go-Shoots," but we were now upon the territory of a far more powerful and warlike tribe, the Piutes. Although we had received no information that the Piutes were on the warpath, it was not fairly dark before signal fires began to glow in various directions from territory which was controlled by that tribe of Indians. It was announced while we had been eating supper that one of our young men who did most of the hunting for our company had wandered off that afternoon with a double-barrelled shotgun in search of game, and had not returned ; the last time he was seen he was skirting the willows more than a mile above camp.

His failure to return to camp before dark, added to the numerous signal fires, gave us notice that our imagined security might be a myth. Orders were at once given to prepare our camp for defense. Our wagons were turned into barricades strengthened by trenches which were hastily dug, as were also rifle pits for outposts. As it was well known that Indians seldom if ever make an attack at the dead of night, we confidently expected an attack, if one were made, at about daybreak. The Indians' method is to approach under cover of the night as near as possible without discovery, hoping to make their assault in the morning a surprise.

While we were busily engaged in digging rifle pits and molding bullets for our guns, our missing hunter suddenly appeared in our midst. He said that while skirting a thicket of basket willows, upon turning a bend he came abruptly upon three Indians in war paint. As was his habit while hunting rabbits or birds with a double-barrelled shotgun, he carried both barrels full cock, and as jack rabbits were difficult of close approach, he used rather heavy shot. The Indians were grouped together at a distance of not more than fifty feet when he first discovered them, and at the same instant they became aware of his presence.

No words were spoken, but our hunter being better prepared for rapid action gave the Indians both barrels of his shotgun at close range before they could bring their guns to bear upon him. Without waiting to ascertain the effect of his volley he immediately wheeled and made several leaps into the basket willows and lay down. He said that it was hardly probable that the Indians he saw were the only ones in that party. If there were others they did not attempt to follow him into the willows, which was commendable discretion on their part. Being armed with a Colt navy revolver in addition to a shotgun our hunter would have made any attempt of the Indians to locate his hiding place rather dangerous, if not indeed disastrous. He had no means of ascertaining the effect of his shots at the original trio, but knowing his skill in the use of a shotgun, we all agreed that those particular Indians would not follow the war path with any great degree of comfort for many weeks to come, if indeed they survived their wounds.

For several hours the young man did not stir from the spot where he first dropped to cover, being fearful that he was surrounded by savages anxious to raise his scalp. This was the reason for his late appearance in our camp. The greatest inconvenience he experienced was from the mosquitoes, of which he said the sloughs along Carson River appeared to have a new variety, with bills long enough to puncture an overshirt.

Before we moved the following morning our camp was visited by a heavily armed party of prospectors. They informed us that the Piute Indians had taken the war path against the whites and that a battle had recently been fought at Pyramid Lake between a company of volunteers and old Winnemucca's band of Piutes. The volunteers, consisting of approximately a hundred men, were commanded by Major Ormsby, a brave but indiscreet man.

The major found the Indians in a position of their own choosing, and immediately gave the order to charge. The attack could only be accomplished by descending a steep winding trail along a rocky sidehill bordered by a rank growth of sagebrush, before gaining the flat where the Indians were camped. Strange as it appears to the present historian, there is no apparent doubt that a charge was ordered before any attempt was made to ascertain the strength of the Indians. The result of this ill-advised charge was what might have been anticipated. It was generally understood that only those who retreated early in the fight, or rather did not fight, but returned to their horses and fled, were the sole survivors of that disastrous fiasco.

When news of the Pyramid Lake disaster arrived at the Presidio, California, an expedition consisting of eight hundred volunteer cavalrymen and two hundred regular infantrymen was dispatched to the scene of the late conflict, to bury the dead and punish the Indians. Arriving on the late battlefield some two weeks later, they found that the Indians, after perpetrating the usual Indian atrocities upon their victims, had separated into small detachments or predatory bands and scattered in every direction, as was well known that they must do for the reason that Winnemucca could not hold together and provide rations for such a large force as he had thrown into the Pyramid Lake battle. The officers of the volunteer cavalry soon learned that pursuit of little bands of Indians through the desert plains of Nevada is a futile waste of energy. Consequently after performing the melancholy part of their mission, burying the victims of the Pyramid Lake battle, retreat was sounded and they returned to division headquarters at San Francisco.

As we had arrived with our train of horses but a few days after the Pyramid Lake battle, it was doubtless one of the predatory bands into which Winnemucca's warriors had separated that encountered our young hunter, causing him to seek shelter in the basket willows. We were informed by our morning callers that we need not anticipate any further interference from the Indians. The valley had been thoroughly scoured by volunteers and all the Indians remaining from Winnemucca's band had been killed or driven off with the possible exception of a few venturesome young warriors, such as our hunter encountered. They were now thoroughly frightened and in hiding, awaiting an opportunity to escape.

Resuming our journey, we arrived that afternoon at Virginia City. This was destined to be the future mining metropolis of Nevada, if not of America. Here our party separated. With those who had joined the horse train at Salt Lake City, I concluded to remain at the embryo Eldorado and seek employment. Those in charge of the horses moved forward to their destined market, San Francisco.

"My partner was a good teacher of mining."

CHAPTER FOUR

TAKING A TURN AT GOLD DIGGING

THERE was plenty of work in Virginia City for willing hands, at what to me appeared fabulous wages. But I was a typical tenderfoot, and the atmosphere of Virginia City, fragrant as it was with the vices of a mining camp, did not appeal to me. Without accepting employment I engaged passage with a party of freighters to Folsom, California. There were two men in this party, each driving four horses hitched to a big freight wagon. At that time, August, 1860, Folsom was the eastern terminus of the railroad which connected with steamboat navigation at Sacramento. Hence all passenger and freight traffic to the new mines at Virginia City and other interior points was transferred by stagecoach or freight wagons from Folsom.

The freighters with, whom I crossed the mountains from Virginia City proved to be partners, not only in freighting but in ownership of a tract of land three miles east of Folsom. This tract they had improved by fencing, planting an orchard, and building a house and barn. When we arrived at Folsom they told me of this place and informed me that I might, if I desired, go out there and live in their house until I found work to do. I would find provisions and a bed in the house, and all they would ask for my occupancy of the place would be for me to feed and water a band of turkeys I would find there and irrigate the orchard once each week. After paying my hotel bill the morning after my arrival at Folsom I took account of my money and found that I had one shiny quarter of a dollar left — twenty-five cents. It is perhaps needless to say that I accepted their offer to give me a stopping place in which to live — without pay, other than liberty to cook my own food.

I discovered that gold mining during the early days in California meant placer mining, and that the placers had been practically exhausted throughout the foothills during the first few years after their discovery. Abandoned cabins, piles of glistening rocks, and wrecked sluice boxes marked the hillsides and gullies, which a few months before teemed with life and energy. During the years of mining activity a company had been organized to pump water on to a piece of ground lying a short distance east of the place where I was living. By means of pumping the water for the sluice boxes, the company had successfully carried on placer mining.

It was found that a few feet below the surface and lying on the bed rock was a stratum of blue clay which was impervious to water. When thrown into the sluice boxes this clay would, under the action of the water, start rolling with the current, and being of a sticky nature would pick up every particle of gold dust with which it came in con-

tact.   It was found also that the loam above the blue clay,
of which there was a depth of from two to four feet, carried
sufficient value in gold to pay for sluicing.   The company
therefore washed off the surface over an area of perhaps
forty acres without disturbing the clay.   Mixed with the
surface loam were a few boulders which were too large
to pass through the sluice boxes; these were piled aside
on the clay.

Just prior to my advent at the ranch a placer miner had
discovered that by picking up the clay and exposing it
to the sun until thoroughly dry, and then treating it to a
water bath, it would slack like lime, and then the gold
dust could be separated from it by the ordinary process
of washing.   It was approximately three miles from this
clay bed to where water might then be obtained, but there
was a good wagon road for the entire distance, and purchasing a horse and dump cart he began his new enterprise.
Building a box similar to the kind plasterers use for
slacking lime, large enough to hold three cartloads, he
would dry and deliver to the box sufficient to fill it; he
would then turn on the water, and while giving it time
to soak and slack would return to the clay bed and spread
out to dry enough to refill his dump, or slacking box.

The second day after taking possession of my location
on the ranch, I came upon him while he was busy spreading
out clay.   As my work there amounted to no more than
a few chores, and the clay beds were so near, it occurred
to me that I might earn an extra dollar by helping to
spread out the clay.   I therefore approached the man,
who proved to be a son of the Emerald Isle, and was immediately engaged at the first offer he made, ten dollars
per week.

My new boss was a bachelor thirty-five years old,
Dennis Dugan by name.   After leaving the "auld sod"

he had resided for several years in Brooklyn, New York. During this period he had met and surrendered his heart to an Irishwoman a few years younger than himself. She refused to marry him, giving as her reason that he had accumulated no money with which to support a wife, although she admitted that she had a tender spot in her heart for him. The first Sunday I was at the ranch he came over and confided that portion of his personal history to me. In concluding the narrative he asked me if I would write a letter for him to his sweet Mary Ann.

He said that when she refused to marry him and he started for California via the Isthmus of Panama, he thought he would die, in fact he wanted to die but could not. Having experienced the pangs of unrequited love a few times when at school in Michigan, my heart went out in sympathy for Dennis, so I consented to write the love letter. The result was that a correspondence was opened between the son and daughter of good old Ireland which eventually terminated in the purchase of another horse and cart, and the marriage of the loving couple.

To successfully conduct the necessary correspondence and eventually deliver the pair over to the priest required several months. In the meantime I found that my sentimental friend Dennis had not confined the supposed secret of his love to me alone, but had confided in others, notably to one Mrs. Patrick Murphy, who in turn related it to Mrs. Teddy Gallagher, who passed it on to Mrs. Malony and Mrs. Keane and by them the intelligence was communicated to Mrs. Jimmy O'Flaherty. In this manner it became commonly known that the newly arrived young man from across the plains was conducting the amatory correspondence for "Dinnis," as my client was popularly called.

The result of this general knowledge was that whenever

I approached the residence of any of the matrons named, some of their numerous progeny would announce the fact. Then the smiling face of the mother appeared before I could pass, and I was greeted with a cheerful "Top of the morning," and "Bless your heart, what news have ye from Brooklyn?" — all this with the invariable assurance, in a whisper, that I might trust her "to kape a secret." Through this fortunate — for Dennis and me — combination of circumstances, I made the acquaintance of the worthy families in the mining camps of "Richmond Hill" and "Mormon Island," Sacramento County, California.

Richmond Hill consisted only of cabins, the residences of families whose men-folks were mining in the near vicinity. It had no stores or shops. Mormon Island was the pathetic spectacle of a mining town after the mines had been exhausted and the miners had fled. It consisted of one main street or road. It boasted of one hotel, one general store, which served the triple purpose of store, post-office, and express office. It was favored with one saloon, named the "Forty Drops." Being a new arrival, a "tenderfoot," and recently from a country where I was not familiar with saloons and saloon etiquette, I used to stare at that sign, and wonder why the saloon was named "Forty Drops," for I soon learned that its patrons did not limit their drinks to forty drops.

For approximately two years after the discovery of gold in paying quantities, Mormon Island was one of the richest mining camps in California. The name had doubtless been given it from the fact that members of the Mormon Battalion, which had helped in the winning of California, had worked here digging the mill race in which James Marshall discovered the gold. Many millions of dollars in gold dust were obtained from the American

River and its adjacent bars and benches in the vicinity of this Island.

I arrived in California during the month of August, 1860, but did not attain my majority until the following month, September 18th. However, the California election law provided that a recently arrived elector's residence dated from the day of his departure from his former home with the intent of making that state his permanent residence. I had started from my home in Michigan April 1, 1860, intending to establish a home in California, therefore I was counted a resident of California from that date, and more than six months having elapsed when the election occurred the following November I was a legal voter and accordingly did vote for the Republican nominee, Abraham Lincoln. The election was conducted in a quiet and orderly manner. While partisan feeling ran high, there were no personal encounters, no unseemly brawls. The next day after the election work of all kinds as well as business proceeded as usual, without a ripple being visible on the surface.

Although the richest of the placer claims were exhausted, many of the original owners of the claims remained. They had erected houses and brought out their families, and in nearly every instance surrounded their buildings with orchards and vineyards. At the time of my arrival the old mining town was a picture of beautifully embowered homes.

Among the families whose acquaintance I had made was one from Australia, named Mulcahy. It consisted of husband, wife, one daughter, and two sons, the younger of whom, Jimmy Mulcahy, was about two years my junior. We proved to have similar likes and dislikes ; consequently we became warm friends. He was an industrious, worthy young man, and if he had acquired any bad habits I never discovered them. He was a thorough sportsman, and the best wing shot I ever knew, which alone was enough to make me love him.

It was through his influence that I first became interested with a placer miner named Cox in a placer claim on American Ridge, about one mile below Mormon Island. I acquired one-half interest in a placer property, which consisted of the ground included in two placer claims, and a miner's cabin sufficiently large to house two men. The furnishings of the cabin were of the simplest and most primitive kind — two narrow bunks, two homemade stools, one small table, and a number seven cook stove, together with a homemade cupboard built against one side of the wall.

The man Cox with whom I had associated myself as a mining partner was of the usual type of American placer miners, a few of whom may yet be found in all placer mining camps along the Pacific Coast. Usually they are ripe in experience — typical "old bachelors," and good cooks of the kind of food to which they have been accustomed. They may not be lazy, but most of them have acquired a tired feeling, which uncharitable persons may mistake for laziness. Mormon Island had for its foremost citizens a coterie of this class of miners.

I was young, physically vigorous, and had not yet acquired the tired feeling. My partner was congenial and a good teacher of mining, but upon me soon fell most of the hard work. However, I was being taught to mine, and did not object, especially as my partner did not appear to be a physically strong man. He proved, however, to be a neat and cleanly housekeeper. After supper every night he would wash and put away the dishes, and then usually suggest that we go to town.

The general resort was the Forty Drops. There we

The "Forty Drops."

would usually find the old bachelor miners, all of whom
preferred assembling at the Forty Drops to spend their
evenings rather than to remain in their lonely, and generally poorly ventilated cabins. Here in the old saloon,
shorn of the glory and hilarity of earlier days, night after
night and usually every afternoon, were seated a silent
group of persons engaged in a game they called "draw."
My partner Cox appeared to enjoy playing this game. As
I became acquainted with the men who frequented that
end of the Forty Drops, the reason dawned upon me why
he and others of his class of miners were always broke.
They did not drink to excess, but they simply contributed
their money to professional gamblers who paid periodical
visits to our camp to collect from their willing victims.

I noticed eventually that the other type of visiting
miners at the Forty Drops seldom or never came back
to the rear of the saloon where cards were being played.
They came in to the bar, usually bought a drink or a cigar,
and after paying for their purchase walked out again.
Those who patronized the card tables were almost invariably American born, and when not engaged in playing
some game of cards indulged in telling stories, or discussing
politics. They were men of varied experience, most of
whom had been born and reared in some of the towns on
the banks of the Mississippi River or its tributaries. Their
number included men of the learned professions as well as

artisans. As may be imagined, the experiences they related were, many of them, of a character to startle and horrify a tenderfoot like myself.

To the credit of these hardened old timers I must say that they never tried to induce me to join them in their social glass, or in their card games. The probable reason for their not asking me to take part in their card games was that they all knew that I had traded my watch and revolver, and paid my last dollar for my interest in our placer claim. My partner Cox was the general manager and treasurer; therefore it was known to every person in the camp that I had no money. The very good reason was that our mine did not yield enough revenue to leave a surplus after Cox's losings at the gaming tables and our modest grocery bills had been paid.

I had not, up to early in December, asked Cox for a statement of our finances. Then he smilingly and in the best humor possible advised me that we had been playing in bad luck; that he had lost in almost every sitting in the game during November, and that we owed the grocer and the butcher for our last month's bills. However, he thought by cleaning up our string of sluices and tail race we would be able to square our debts. The next morning we accordingly cleaned up everything, and fortunately as he had predicted, we found enough gold dust to settle all our debts. He then proposed to me that we sever our mining partnership; or rather that he would quit and turn over the claim, cabin, tools, and mining oufit to me. I accepted his proposition.

A few days later I joined my fortunes with a little Irishman named Johnny Cauley. He had located a hydraulic claim on Richmond Hill, which had been worked and abandoned some years before, when only such a claim as would pay from five to ten dollars per day was considered

worth working. We transferred the mining tools and fix-
tures, including several hundred feet of canvas hose, from
the Cox claim on Maple Ridge to the Richmond Hill property, and began sluicing operations at once.

The ground had been worked back from the rim rock
until a depth of over twenty feet of gravel had been gained
before the former claimants had abandoned the property.
The larger boulders and coarser gravel were thrown back
from the bank as the work progressed, leaving a cleared
space upon which the bank from time to time, as under-
mined by force of the water thrown from the hydraulic,
would cave, frequently in great masses. Upon this material
a stream of water would be directed from the hose and
pipe. All the soil and fine gravel would be washed from
the boulders and coarser gravel, and carried off through
a rim-rock tunnel. This tunnel was equipped with sluice
boxes and ripples charged with quicksilver to catch the
gold dust.

The strenuous part of our work was to move back the
heavy gravel or rocks. We had to keep sufficient space
clear to properly handle the next cave of the bank. This
we accomplished by starting a wall of the heaviest rocks at
the extreme outside of the space heretofore kept open. As
we added to its height we threw the other or lighter bowl-
ders behind the face wall. We built up terrace above
terrace by passing on the rocks, after being washed clean,
from one terrace to another.

My first winter in California, thus spent, proved to be
more profitable in developing our muscles than in adding
to our little hoard of gold dust. We kept all the dust concealed in a Preston and Merrill yeast-powder can. Yet
though it had not made me rich in money returns, I have
always recalled with pleasure the winter I spent on Richmond Hill. Early in May, 1861, I bade good-by to the

many friends I had made in that old California gold-mining camp. The good-hearted folk — men, women, and children — I had met there had shown a real friendship for me in their own interesting ways.

"To accompany the children home involved a long walk."

CHAPTER FIVE

TEACHING SCHOOL IN OLD OREGON

DURING the summer of '61 rumors of fabulous gold discoveries on the Salmon and Clearwater rivers in Idaho began to penetrate California, and a general stampede ensued. Catching the "Salmon River fever," I arranged my business affairs early in May, 1862, and took passage on the passenger coach at midnight from Dutch Flat for Folsom. There I connected with the railroad for Sacramento, and from there took passage on a river steamboat to San Francisco.

Arriving there after dark, I secured a cab to convey me to the "What Cheer House." For this service the courteous cab driver charged me $2.50. I was told by the office clerk upon registering that a city ordinance fixed cab fare from the boats to the hotels at $1.50, but to avoid discovery the driver stopped his cab, and landed me half a block from the hotel entrance, where he could collect

"The steerage was crowded with the most heterogeneous assemblage
of human beings I had ever been thrown among."

his fare without observation and interference from the
hotel management.   That was my first ride in a city cab,
and my first lesson in city ways and means.

Upon inquiry I learned that the *Sierra Nevada*, a steamship plying between San Francisco and Portland, Oregon,
was to sail the second day after my arrival.   As I had
never seen an ocean-going steamer, I thought it would
be well to visit the dock where she lay to arrange for my
passage.   When I arrived at the wharf I made inquiry
and was shown through the cabin and steerage.   The
down cargo had been discharged the day before, and the
steerage had been thoroughly renovated by hot water and
steam until the air below the hatches was perfect;   no
disagreeable odor was perceptible.   Upon applying at the
office to purchase my ticket, I was informed that the fare
in the cabin to Portland was forty dollars, while the steerage fare was only twenty.   The voyage from San Francisco to Portland, I was told, would be no more than three

days, therefore the difference between first and second class transportation meant a saving of at least six dollars a day while on board the ship. My early training in economy decided the question: I bought a steerage ticket.

When the ship left her dock the following day I was one of several hundred passengers on their way to the new Eldorado. The steerage was crowded with the most heterogeneous assemblage of human beings I had ever been thrown among. Too late I regretted that I had economized in purchasing my ticket. The air soon became foul, both morally and physically; profanity, tobacco smoke, and the fumes of garlic and bad whisky combined to render that voyage, at least to me, never to be forgotten. The weather during the entire trip continuing favorable, we made what was then considered a record trip. Fifty-four hours after leaving the San Francisco dock we entered the mouth of the Columbia River.

Portland at that time was a comparatively small city, inadequately provided with hotels to accommodate the large number of travelers passing through its portals on their way to what were termed the "Salmon River Mines." I managed to find in another "What Cheer House," how-ever, a cot void of sheets or pillow case. The "What Cheer House," like all other hotels in the city, was filled to the limit. The tide of travel was now setting in both ways. While the stronger current was running to the mines, yet large numbers of disappointed prospectors were trying to make their way back to their former homes.

The conversation of the disappointed prospectors set me thinking. It occurred to me that it might be best for me to return to San Francisco on the same steamer on which I had come. The next morning I went down to the steamer wharf to book a passage back to San Francisco.

While I was watching the crew discharge cargo, two men,

apparently farmers, came down to the dock to see the ship. One of the men, as I learned afterward, was familiarly called "Whispering Griner," for the reason that when conversing in his usual tone of voice he could be heard at a distance of a full city block or more. Consequently I overheard their conversation, and became deeply interested in their remarks. One of them incidentally mentioned "Yamhill" as the country from which they came. That name aroused my curiosity, as I had never heard it spoken before. When I learned that the place was in Oregon, the thought occurred to me, why not go out to Yamhill, instead of returning to California?

I approached and began questioning the men about Yamhill. They willingly gave me all the information they possessed about the extreme West. Both had crossed the plains with ox teams, bringing their families and household goods with them before any buildings had been erected on the site where the city of Portland stood.

I asked them if any schools had been started in Yamhill. They answered in the affirmative, and told me that there was a vacancy at that time in their district; the school trustees were anxious to find a teacher. They invited me to ride out with them, stating that their teams and wagons were at a feed yard at the upper end of First Street. Having determined to accept their invitation, I transferred my baggage to their wagons.

While waiting for the time when my new-found friends should start for Yamhill, I took a stroll through the streets of pioneer Portland. The town, I found, had been located in a dense forest on a bend of the Willamette River, which was navigable for ocean steamers up to that point. The trees back from the river had been chopped down and removed from the first three streets, which were plotted parallel with the river. The stumps had been completely cleared away from none except Front Street; and only for a distance of a few blocks along that, which was the principal business street. The "stumping" of Portland's streets was a herculean task. The fir timber grew to an immense size and close together on the ground. A public school had already been provided. The pupils as I passed were assembling after the noon recess. Their healthy and vigorous appearance bore out a remark made by a fellow-passenger while the steamer upon which I came up the Columbia River was breasting the current, that "Oregon is the land of big red apples and rosy-cheeked girls."

The hour having arrived which the farmers had set for our departure, I joined them at the feed corral. We were soon on our way up what they called the "cañon road." It was a gradual and easy grade up this cañon for a distance of three or four miles to the summit of the Portland Heights. Arriving there, we found a large two-story dwelling house on the right-hand side of the road, and across the highway from the house was a large open shed, erected for the accommodation of farmers and others who desired to camp at that point, a moderate charge being made for the shelter. Immediately behind the shed was a dense forest of native firs. The road we were to follow the next day had been hewn through this otherwise impenetrable forest.

We arrived in the valley of the Yamhill during the afternoon. I was surprised to find what appeared to be an old farming community. But little more than a decade had elapsed since the first white settlers had located in that valley, yet each 640 acres was surrounded by a substantial "stake and rider" fence. The houses and barns were similar to those seen in the New England states, with the one observable difference, the lack of paint, which was seldom obtainable by the first settlers in Oregon. The roofs of the buildings wore an appearance of age, being covered with moss, with which the trees were also festooned. This was the result of excessive rainfall there during the winter months.

Both my friends invited me to their homes. I accepted the invitation of the one with whom I chanced to be riding, promising the other a visit the next day, and offering to help him mark and brand some young cattle he had recently bought.

My mind had been made up to apply for the vacant position of teacher in the district, and that plan was carried out. During Monday, after keeping my promise to help with the cattle, I saw the trustees of the school district, and contracted to teach their school six months for thirty dollars a month and board. The board was to be obtained by boarding around at the homes of the pupils.

The next Tuesday I visited the county seat, Lafayette. Here I interviewed the Superintendent of Schools, passed the teachers' examination, and obtained a certificate. Then I returned to the home and farm of one of the trustees, familiarly known as "Uncle Johnnie Perkins." He and his wife were natives of New York State. With several relatives they had crossed the plains during the summer of 1845, and located homesteads under the original Oregon homestead act. They had all prospered, and as I learned later, were among the wealthiest farmers in the county.

The schoolhouse, I found, was an old frame building which had never been painted, and the shingles on the roof were covered with moss. The windows were of 8 by 10 sash, but most of the glass had been broken. The interior, if possible, was more gloomy than the exterior. The desks and seats with which the schoolroom was furnished were of the home manufacture common in frontier schoolrooms. A large box stove was supplied for heating the room and, when necessary, drying the garments of the pupils. It was coated with rust, as it had never been polished.

The building was pleasantly located on an elevation overlooking a beautiful valley dotted with homes. The site had evidently been donated by one or more of the settlers in the school district. The public highway skirted one side of the school tract, most of which was thrown open, and was a resort for stray cattle and horses. However, the highest point of the tract, about five acres, where the schoolhouse was erected, was inclosed by a substantial fence. No gate was provided for entrance to this inclosure, but strong, wide steps were constructed from the ground on the inner and outer side to a broad platform on top of the fence. This provided easy entrance to the schoolhouse, without the possible risk of neglecting to shut a gate.

Returning to the Perkins home, I reported to "Uncle Johnnie" the condition in which I had found the schoolhouse. I further told him that I would provide the money to buy glass for the windows, and a few maps and pictures of historical interest to decorate the walls of the schoolroom. As it chanced he was planning to go to Portland the next day, and would return Friday evening. We planned therefore to glaze the windows on Saturday, scrub out the building, hang the pictures and have the room in readiness to begin school on Monday.

When our labors were completed Saturday evening the schoolroom presented a fairly attractive appearance, with the exception of the old rusty stove. It dawned upon me that the stove might be hid by covering it with wild roses which grew in profusion on the upper end of the school ground and in the fence corners along the road; they were in full bloom at that particular time, and I could gather some before the pupils arrived. I came early on Monday morning and worked industriously until the old rusty stove was a bank of flowers and the room redolent with the perfume of roses. Thus my first term of school in Oregon had a pleasant and cheerful beginning.

. All the boys and girls of school age living within the boundaries of that school district became my pupils. Several others who were nonresidents also gained permission to attend. The parents of those young people, both fathers and mothers, had crossed the plains, braving all the dangers that journey involved, to establish a new commonwealth, and rear their children to lives of industry and freedom. Their intense desire to give their sons and daughters the benefits of an education was proved to me by the fact that though both seedtime and harvest occurred during my first school term of six months, in not a single instance was either boy or girl required to remain at home to help at the extra work.

As evidence of the salubrity of the climate, and the physical vigor of the Oregon pioneers, of the sixty pupils enrolled on my school roster none was reported as absent on account of illness. In the matter of dress, the girls were guided by the vigorous common sense of their mothers. They wore no high-heeled shoes nor silk stockings. It must not be imagined by the young men and women of today that the sons and daughters of the early pioneers were dowdy in appearance, for quite the reverse was the case. They were neat, clean, and earnest. One of my pupils, a young lady nineteen years old, lived with her father and mother at a distance of three miles from the school, yet she walked those three miles every morning before school began, and walked back in the evening after school was dismissed. This distance of six miles she

" I continued to make my principal abiding place with the Perkins family."

traveled every day for six months, without being absent at any roll call.   It is extremely doubtful if our schoolgirls of today who wear high-heeled shoes could maintain such a record.

In boarding around with my pupils, I soon discovered that my lot had been cast in a most hospitable community. True, to accompany the pupils home frequently involved a long walk, but a cordial welcome was always given me, and the younger pupils were so clamorous for me to go home with them that I was usually engaged several evenings in advance.   As I seldom accompanied the children of any one family home more than one night at a time, the distances I was required to travel varied.   I continued, however, to make my principal abiding place with the Perkins family.

Uncle Johnnie, his wife, and the boys and girls were a typical hard-working pioneer family.   During the summer months all were up and dressed ready for action at 5 : 30. Uncle Johnnie and his hired men — never less than one, and often three or four — began their labor for the day by hastening to the barn to feed and harness the horses.   The mother, aided by her two daughters, meanwhile prepared breakfast; and the two younger boys drove in the cows from the pasture. Promptly at 6 : 30 breakfast was announced, and hurriedly gathering around the family table every head was bowed while a blessing was invoked. There was no unseemly hurry or confusion, but breakfast was quickly eaten. Then the men went out for their work. The girls and their brothers, with glistening tin pails, started for the corrals. They milked fourteen cows the summer I was there; the buckets, brimful of milk, were carried to the dairy house. Then came washing the breakfast dishes, making up the beds, and sweeping all the rooms, before preparing for school. All this work was accomplished day after day, with never a tardy mark against them. In addition to the tasks named, the family washing was done by the girls every Saturday.

The state of Kentucky is justly famous for the number of colonels it has developed; the state of Oregon may refer with pride to the number and character of her "Uncles," none of whom was related by ties of blood to his nieces or nephews. We recognized as uncles, in the school district in which I featured, "Uncle John Perkins," who was a Yankee from New York, "Uncle Tom Davis," who crossed the plains from Missouri, and "Uncle Jimmie Burton," an Englishman from Australia, who having become naturalized, was a loyal American citizen. In addition to the foregoing uncles, I might enumerate "Uncle Caleb Wood," "Uncle Doc Sitton" and "Uncle Andy Wright," all of whom, with many others, were freeholders under the Oregon homestead act.

Soon after my school began I was informed that great "doin's" were to be had in a grove on "Uncle Tom Davis' " land on the Fourth of July. During the evening and night of that eventful day there was to be a big dance at the home of "Uncle John Perkins." The "doin's" in the grove were to include a picnic dinner, patriotic music, an address by a local orator, and a general reunion of the old pioneers, who would be present from long distances up the valley. The arrangements for the celebration completed, the tidings were sent out on the first of the month. During the days intervening between the announcement and the Fourth, every kitchen in the neighborhood was redolent with the aroma of baking pies, cakes, and other eatables that were being prepared for the picnic dinner. Those intervening three days appeared to my pupils as never-ending; but eventually the sun rose on a cloudless sky the morning of the Fourth, and the great day had arrived.

The grove in which the exercises of the day were to be held was about two miles from the Perkins home. As there were no carriages or buggies in the country at that time, saddle horses supplied the deficiency. On that morning a band of horses was driven in from the pasture; and every man, woman, boy, and girl brought forth from its storage a saddle. Each member of the family had soon caught and saddled his or her particular horse. Then came a demonstration of horsemanship which revealed that the Oregon girls were equestriennes of ability and skill. There were no tardy attendants that day. Flurries of dust on the highways in many directions announced the gathering of squadrons of riders to the place of celebration. The grove was soon resplendent with blue and pink ribbons and white dresses.

That assemblage of pioneers with their sons and daughters was a unit in its desire to fittingly commemorate the establishment of this Republic, and no word was uttered to mar the harmony of the patriotic gathering. After the speaking, which was followed by vocal selections, including

"America," and "Nearer my God to Thee," came the picnic dinner. And in the evening the dance came off, as planned, at the Perkins home. To say that "joy was unconfined" would be but feebly to express the hilarity of the occasion. Young and old in wholesome spirit mingled together, the older ones chatting and visiting while their boys and girls danced. So closed what seems one of the happiest of all of the celebrations among the many in which I have been privileged to participate. Indeed, looking back through a lapse of more than half a century, I see it all as though it were but yesterday; and I cannot recall another like occasion in which the good fellowship was so general. The participants were all like one happy family.

This was characteristic of those Oregon pioneers. In the masterly work they performed of confirming the Nation's title to that vast empire of the far Northwest, and in carving out and organizing the splendid states not only of Oregon but Washington, Idaho, and parts of others out of the Oregon Territory, they worked unitedly. I feel it imperative in closing this chapter dealing with my experiences as a pioneer teacher among them to pay this tribute to the heroes and the heroines who performed this signal service for our country with such whole-hearted American spirit. No words of mine can ever praise those noble men and women enough.

The wives and mothers are deserving of especial credit. The men were brave and industrious, but neither in bravery nor industry did they excel the brave women who stood by their side throughout those arduous days of pioneering. I speak advisedly when I say that they were good cooks, capable and industrious housewives, kind and affectionate mothers, and benevolent and charitable neighbors. I had an opportunity not only to test their skill as cooks, but to observe their patience and Christian benevolence.   Children reared under such parentage will prove a fitting bulwark against discord and danger to their state and general government, if an emergency should ever arise.

"The packs were secured by the diamond hitch, and off we set on
our new venture."

CHAPTER SIX

ON TO BOISÉ BASIN

My second engagement as teacher came to a pleasant close.
Then I was offered again the position as teacher in the
Perkins district, at the same salary I had received the
former year. I had other plans, however, which made me
decline the offer. News of rich discoveries of gold in the
Boisé Basin in Idaho had filtered into Oregon. I was
eager now to gain sufficient wealth to establish a home of
my own, to which I might invite as a companion and life-
long partner one of Oregon's fair daughters. But in discussing my plans I did not reveal to my friends that my
ambition had taken such a lofty flight.

In California I had discovered that all those men who
had truck gardens in the vicinity of the mines made money
surely and rapidly. If they did not get drunk and play
poker, they got rich. Since I had not acquired those bad
habits, I concluded that this would be an easy road to
realize my dreams.

On beginning a canvass among my acquaintances to find
a suitable young man for a partner, I soon discovered that
I did not rate very high in that community as an agricul-

turist. Being a school teacher, I was called a "Horace
Greeley farmer." It happened, however, that a Canadian,
a miller by trade, had come into the neighborhood from
Caribou. The previous fall he had found employment
running a local flouring mill. When I approached him on
the subject of gardening and had explained my plans, he
agreed to join me, for the reason that he was not making
any money at his then employment.

We proceeded at once to take account of our money,
and found that each had about three hundred and fifty
dollars. This I believed would, by the exercise of prudence, be sufficient to purchase six pack animals and their
equipment, together with garden seeds, and supplies to
carry us through. After several conferences at which the
details of our proposed venture were discussed, he handed
over to me his money, telling me to put it with mine, and
buy such things as we would need, while he would continue to run the mill until I was ready to start.

My newly acquired partner, John Porter, was a fine
specimen of physical manhood, a few years older than I.
He was an English-Canadian by birth and inheritance, and
I doubt if Her Majesty the Queen of England had a more
loyal subject throughout her realm. He knew little or
nothing about any other employment than milling, but he
was willing to learn, and good natured. Like all English-
men whom I have known, he was a good walker. As I had
training in that line while boarding around with my pupils
in Oregon, we determined to economize by walking, and
thus avoid the expense of purchasing saddle horses.

Neither of us had learned the art of throwing on the
diamond hitch, commonly used by packers. Realizing
that this was absolutely necessary, I got a packer named
Brooks to train me. Day after day until ready to put the
instructions he gave me into actual practice, I kept saying

over in my mind, "This rope goes this way, that rope goes that way." Finally the practical test came, April 1, 1863, when part of our animals had to be loaded with potatoes, intended for seed, and flour for our commissary. The packs were secured by the diamond hitch as securely and quickly as if we were old followers of the trail, and off we set on our new venture.

It was a beautiful spring day. The winter had been unusually mild; consequently the fruit trees were in blossom. As we approached the town of Hillsboro, in passing through a narrow lane embowered on both sides with trees in full bloom, I remarked to Porter, "This is a beautiful town."

A voice from behind the trees responded, "Yes, young man, and it is a great pity, you will never see it again. The Indians on Burnt River will take the scalps of the last one of you men who are attempting to reach Boisé."

I must admit that this salutation came like a douche of cold water, but it had no deterrent effect upon our purpose to push forward.

We remained the first night out, April 1, 1863, at Hillsboro. The following day during the forenoon we arrived at Portland. Here we completed our purchases, including the irons of a plow. Being novices in the art of packing we hesitated to attempt to pack the beam and handles. We also purchased a pair of collars and hames, intending to improvise a set of harness out of the ropes we used in lashing on our packs.

That same afternoon we shipped our supplies, including our pack animals and ourselves, to The Dalles, Oregon, by the O. S. N. line of river boats. These boats could not ascend the Columbia River farther than the Cascades. From there all freight and passengers for up-river points were transferred to other boats, which ran between the upper Cascades and The Dalles. The portage, which was approximately three miles, was accomplished by a horse tramway on a wooden track. Over this the passengers and freight were conveyed. Loose animals were driven by their owners across the portage, from the lower to the upper boats. Meals of excellent quality at a reasonable price were served on both boats. Our day on the Columbia River passed off without any startling occurrence, and we arrived about 6 P.M. at The Dalles, making a landing on the sand beach below the Umatilla House.

During our passage up the river we met a young man whom we knew in the valley. As he too had started to walk to the new Boisé discoveries, we invited him to join us. He gladly accepted the invitation. As soon as the horses were landed we drove them out to Three-Mile Creek. We were told this was the nearest camping ground at which grass and water could be had for our animals. The night passed off quietly, and the following morning, after partaking of a hearty breakfast consisting of bannocks of bread baked in a frying pan before the camp fire, fat bacon, and black coffee, we started back to the river at The Dalles, driving our horses before us.

Arriving at the boat, we found that our supplies had been landed in a pile apart from the general cargo. Then, if not before, we appreciated the value of having our young Oregon friend, Bill Dixon, to assist us in rounding up and packing the animals. While engaged at that rather arduous task, we were favored by the presence of at least fifty "rubbernecks." Men of all nationalities and shades of color gathered to watch us and proceeded to criticize Oregon and all Oregonians, especially all denizens of Yamhill. We quickly lashed the cargo on our pack animals, and without reply or retort to any of their witticisms, "hit the trail" for the Boisé country.

Our progress across the Deschutes River and up Rock Creek was uninterrupted. We soon arrived at the Umatilla Reservation at the point where the Oregon Trail emerges from the Blue Mountains. Here we learned that there had been a heavy fall of snow on the summit of the mountains but a few weeks prior to our arrival, increasing the depth of the snow on the summit, at Meacham, to approximately five feet. However, we heard that a pack trail had been broken through, to permit the passage of saddle animals. We started up the western slope of the mountain early one morning, and upon reaching the snow line found the trail well broken. The snow was several feet in depth, as had been reported, but in the vicinity of the Meacham roadhouse, it was beaten down and packed by saddle and pack animals, which were at that time crossing the summit in great numbers.

Immediately we set about preparing a camp for the night. Our horses were relieved of their packs, and tied in a line to a lash rope fastened between two fir trees. How to build a fire sufficient to cook supper on top of such deep snow would have probably seemed like a difficult problem, had not those who camped there the previous night left behind them proof of its solution. They had felled a fir tree about six inches in diameter, and cutting the trunk of the tree into lengths of about five feet, had placed these side by side upon the snow, like a corduroy road, until they had a platform sufficiently large to accommodate their fire.

They had made further use of the tree they had felled by trimming off its top branches. By sticking the butt ends of these branches into the snow and leaning the tops at a similar angle, all in the same direction, and by covering the boughs with blankets, they had made a very comfortable spring bed. We were apt pupils, and following the example set before us, we quickly prepared supper, and made down our beds, or rather bed, for we were bedfellows as well as traveling companions.

To get an early start we retired early, and being fatigued were soon asleep, with the stars shining brightly above us. Every sign indicated a clear night; but a few hours later we were awakened by snowflakes falling upon our faces. Instinctively we drew the blankets over our heads, and without loss of time were soon asleep again. When daylight came, we awoke to find spread over us a blanket of snow several inches in depth; but it only helped to make our bed warmer.

While breakfast was being prepared, the horses were fed and saddled. Anticipating a snow camp, we had brought with us a sack of oats for our horses. This we made to serve for their evening and morning feed. Very soon we were on our way for a lower altitude where grass could be found for our horses. The following night we camped on the bank of the Grand-Ronde River, below the snow line.

Next day we arrived at La Grande, then a village of several hundred inhabitants. A majority of them were emigrants who had crossed the plains the previous summer to escape the horrors of the Civil War, then ravaging the states from which they came, Missouri and Arkansas. La Grande, being the only town of any considerable size west of the recently discovered Boisé and Owyhee mines, was a temporary abiding place for travelers to rest, obtain information, and renew their supplies.

We made our camp at the upper end of the village. Our animals we turned out to graze on the foothills east of town, the snow having disappeared in that quarter. The rank growth of bunch grass there was badly bleached, but was a luxury to our half-starved animals.

New arrivals from Boisé Basin told us that the Indians between Powder River and Snake River along the Burnt River trail were running off a great many horses and mules. No open attack had yet been made on travelers, but there was a general feeling of distrust, causing extra precautions to be taken by those who were on their way to the mines. Travelers passing through that region should be heavily armed, they advised, and guards should be maintained over camps at night.

In purchasing our outfit at Portland, we had neglected to provide ourselves with firearms. We concluded that it might be wise to provide at least two of our party with guns. We failed to find in the stores any such merchandise; but eventually we were fortunate enough to be able to purchase a couple of muzzle loading rifles from men who were going to Portland. Having passed the danger zone, they were willing to sell their guns. They had a sufficient supply of ammunition, which they turned over to us with the guns.

That afternoon, while rounding up our horses, our man Dixon found, in the tall bunch grass, a Colt revolver. It had evidently been lost there months before. It was fully loaded in every chamber, but so badly rusted that the cylinder would not revolve, and the hammer could not be raised. However, it presented possibilities, and Dixon declared that he would remove the charges and restore the action of the weapon at the first good camp we made.

Having written letters to our friends, we packed our animals the second morning after our arrival at La Grande. Then following the Oregon Trail toward the east, we crossed the divide which separates Grande-Ronde from Powder River Valley, making the ascent at Ladd's station. After reaching the summit we found the road on the eastern side was a gentle decline until we arrived at a beautiful little valley, which drained into Powder River. Here we camped, unloaded our animals, and turned them loose to graze. The wind was blowing such a stiff gale that we found it impracticable to build a fire and do any cooking above the surface. We soon had a bed of coals in a pit, and without difficulty prepared our meal.

After the usual formality of washing the dishes, Dixon brought forth his find, the revolver. He proposed to restore it to a condition in which it would be effective to shoot horse thieves, or other lawless persons. While he was thus engaged and Porter was preparing his odorous pipe for a good smoke, I concluded that I would walk up to where our horses were grazing, and turn them back toward camp. I had just reached my destination when I heard a pistol shot. Turning around to look, I saw both Dixon and Porter lying flat on the ground, rolling away from the camp fire. At the same instant I heard another shot, and then another, while both the men continued to roll rapidly away from the fire.

I was told later, after quiet was restored, that Dixon had concluded to melt the bullets out of his revolver. It apparently did not occur to him that although the revolver had, from appearance, lain out in the weather many weeks if not months, yet the powder was in as perfect condition as when the pistol was loaded. To carry out his object he had detached the cylinder from the revolver, and dropped it into the glowing bed of coals. The method adopted by Dixon certainly removed the bullets. The first explosion threw the cylinder several feet in the air; as it dropped back into the coals another charge exploded with similar results, until the entire six chambers were discharged. Before the last shot was exploded Porter and Dixon had rolled several rods from the fire. Fortunately they both escaped injury.

We moved on into Powder River Valley the next day, and finally arrived at Burnt River. The water in it was so high that the several crossings usually made in passing up or down the stream were impracticable. Following a high-water trail on the north and west side of the river for several miles, we eventually came to a bridge, so called, which had been made by falling a tree across the stream, and pinning a pole on each side near the top, which had been flattened by chopping off the bark.

This structure was presided over by a very capable-appearing genius, armed with two six-shooters and an effective-looking cheese knife. He informed us that the toll for crossing his bridge was one dollar each for pack animals, and the same for footmen. Without argument we contributed nine dollars to his exchequer, and proceeded on our way.

A continual stream of travel was coming and going through the Burnt River cañon. We experienced no interference, however, from Indians or renegade whites during our passage through that country. Following the old Oregon Trail, we camped at "Tub Springs," arriving the next day at Washoe Ferry on Snake River, where we crossed into the newly created Territory of Idaho. From that crossing we hurried on up the Payette Valley, and on the evening of April 30, 1863, just one month after our departure from Yamhill, Oregon, we camped on a small stream which emptied into the Payette River approximately three miles above Horseshoe Bend on that stream.

We had emerged from the region of sagebrush, and entered a land of bunch grass and buttercups. The evening of our arrival was redolent with the perfume of flowers. All that makes the springtime the most delightful season of the year was there to give cheer. Our camp was pitched about a hundred yards below the point where the trail crossed the creek. Above us, as far as the eye could reach, the smoke from dozens of camp fires was visible. It was but thirteen miles, we learned, to Boisé Basin, and we were on the main-traveled trail. After supper, while Porter and Dixon were enjoying their after-dinner smoke, I concluded that our horses were feeding too far away from camp, so I followed to turn them back. On returning to camp, I said, "Here, Porter, we will drive our stakes."

"Do you think so?" said he.

"Yes," I replied; "this creek rises in yonder high mountain, and consequently there will be water in it all summer, sufficient to irrigate our garden. There is enough land on this bottom for our purpose, in fact more than we have seed to plant."

The following day we found that three other locations had been made on a creek about a mile to the north. Two of them were made by parties who had crossed the plains the summer before, bringing with them ox teams and the necessary appliances, including a few garden seeds, to begin farming on a moderate scale. I visited their camps and found that they had broken up more land than they had seed to plant. At once I made a bargain with both parties under which we secured the use of their surplus land, together with sufficient water to irrigate it.

This fortunate arrangement made it possible for us to plant our potatoes the next day after our arrival. We also secured the service of a man, team, and plow to break up and prepare for planting two acres on our location. This was immediately planted in garden vegetables. At the time we purchased our outfit and garden seeds in Portland, there were no onion sets in that market, but fortunately I had secured from an old lady in Yamhill a milk pan full, or about six quarts. These were the first to be planted, Porter having prepared sufficient ground by spading.

The creek upon which we located was a mountain stream having a heavy fall. We were therefore able to divert water for irrigating our garden, by digging a short ditch. The soil of the creek bottom proved to be a rich sandy loam, well adapted for raising vegetables, and in a few weeks gave promise of a full reward for our labors.

"Three men arose from the laurel and demanded a halt."

CHAPTER SEVEN

PLEASANT AND UNPLEASANT PEDDLING EX-PERIENCES

IT was not long before we were beginning to prosper in our new venture, but with prosperity came a train of unfamiliar experiences, both pleasant and unpleasant. It was a new, wild community in which we had cast our lots for better or for worse. We soon had a taste of both phases of the life.

The onion sets Porter and I had planted first made a rank growth. I pulled them all one morning, and having tied them in bunches of one dozen each, found that we had one hundred bunches of very toothsome-looking green onions. Saddling a couple of our horses, I loaded the onions on one of them, and riding the other, I started for Placerville. Upon my arrival I opened my pack of onions and immediately was surrounded by a crowd of men, all clamorous to secure some. Within an hour I had sold them all at one dollar a bunch, — an even one hundred dollars for the product of a large pan of onion sets.

The result of this sale was soon known to our neighboring ranchers. I learned that two acres of ground on one of the places from which we had rented land had been sown with onion seed. The onions had come up in splendid shape, but looked as if they would be a failure. One of the men who was associated in planting these onions, and who owned a fourth interest in the garden, was a "down-East" Yankee. Having been reared on a farm, he realized that their seed onions were drying up, and would prove a failure. He offered to sell to me his fourth interest in the onions for the hundred dollars I had received for the onions in Placerville. After making a bargain that if I bought his interest, one fourth of the two acres, or one-half acre, would be measured off, that I might have full control of it, I paid him the one hundred dollars, and my portion of the onion patch was measured off, and assigned to me.

The ground upon which the onions were sown was a light, sandy loam, sloping very gradually toward the river. The seed having been sown early, while the ground was damp, had come up well, but as the season advanced the topsoil dried out, and the delicate plants did not possess sufficient vitality to send their roots down to where moisture still remained, consequently they were wilted. Water they must have. None of the men who crossed the plains the previous summer, and who were now attempting to raise a garden in Idaho, knew anything about irrigation.

My first experience on a ranch in California now came to my relief. I immediately proceeded to dig a ditch around the outside lines of my half acre, using the dirt to form a dyke, or embankment, similar to the ring in a circus. After this was completed I turned the water from the irrigating ditch on to the onions and let it run until the entire surface of the half acre was covered, keeping it covered until the ground was thoroughly soaked. I then turned the water off.

The result was marvelous. In a few days the ground appeared to be covered with green onions. Two weeks later I repeated the treatment; and four weeks from the time I gave the little spindling onions their first bath, I thinned a few of the thickest patches by removing one hundred dozen. These I sold as readily as I had the others. Their removal was hardly missed. The result of the purchase of that half acre of wilted onions was a net profit to my partner and myself of one thousand dollars.

The owners of the remainder of the two acres followed our example and irrigated their holdings. They preferred to allow the young onions to attain their full growth, rather than to dispose of them while green; consequently we enjoyed a monopoly of the market for green onions. Radishes and lettuce soon followed the appearance of green onions on the market. They were sold in small bunches at twenty-five cents a bunch.

It was a high-priced market we had entered. Early potatoes first brought forty-five cents a pound; early beets, tops and all, netted the same price as early potatoes; cucumbers were two dollars a dozen, green corn two dollars a dozen ears; tomatoes, forty-five cents per pound, early York cabbage, about half mature, brought seventy-five cents a pound; watermelons were twenty-five cents a pound. From the foregoing market report, which applies to the summer and fall of 1863, it will be seen that the pioneer farmers who located and pursued their calling within reach of the market created by the Boisé mines were engaged in a more certain, if not more profitable employment than actual mining.

Our market for this produce in the beginning was Placerville, the new mining camp. Some four weeks after our arrival, on the completion of our first planting, I had paid this place a visit to see it and to prospect for business.

I still keep in vivid memory the experiences of that day.

It was on a Sunday morning I rode up the trail that had been graded up the steepest part of the mountain to the camp. The trail had not been built by public enterprise, for at the thickest part of the timber, where a little spring came trickling down the hill, I found a gate. Here a very capable-looking man, armed with the usual complement of revolvers, directed my attention to the rate of toll, fifty cents each for saddle animals. This moderate levy I cheerfully paid, and finished by journey.

This first visit to Boisé Basin was during the month of May, 1863, about nine months after the first discovery of gold in that region. Although winter was included in that time, and the annual fall of snow at that altitude is usually from four to six feet, four towns had sprung into existence. All these were busy hives of industry and enterprise. Considering that up to that time all supplies were brought from steamboat landings on the Columbia River, on pack horses and mules, and the only conveyance for passengers was saddle animals, it seemed as if the Basin must have been touched by some magician's wand. But it was gold that worked the charm.

Placerville was originally built with a plaza in the center. Facing it on all sides were stores, saloons, and various other business houses. As I rode down Granite Street on to the plaza, the impression I received will always remain engraved upon my memory. It was Sunday, and the miners from adjacent gulches were in town to buy supplies, or seeking amusement. In front of a saloon on the north side of the plaza, a dense crowd had assembled.

"It was Sunday, and the miners from adjacent gulches were
in town."

With the proverbial curiosity of the tenderfoot, I pushed
my way into the crowd. Gaining the attention of a man
who stood by, I asked him what caused the excitement.
"Oh nothing," he replied, "man for breakfast, that's all.
They have moved him into the shade of the saloon." He
pointed around the corner. Following his direction, I
ventured with others to take a look. There, sure enough,
lying on the ground was "Hickey," a former member of
the notorious gang of robbers and murderers who had for
two preceding years terrorized Lewiston, Florence, and
other mining camps in the north.

Accompanied by some of his former boon companions,
"Hickey" had made his way to the Basin. Although the
quality of the whisky obtainable at that early period was
not so enlivening as later brews, it was sufficient to give
him the courage to attempt to "run a bluff" on an old-
timer known by the euphonious name of "Snapping
Andy." Andy proved to have too much snap. Snatch-
ing a pick handle from a barrel conveniently near, he gave

"Hickey" his quietus before the latter could use his revolver. The skull was indented where the blow took effect. The body was permitted to lie there all that day.

This was the first of many tragedies which came to my notice during the early days in Boisé Basin. Boy and tenderfoot that I was, for many months I could not banish from my mind that lifeless form. Even now, as I pen these lines, I can see it all again, — the bearded men, the roofs steep-pitched to shed the snow, the lofty trees, and around all the eternal hills — mute witnesses to the tragedy.

A short time previous to the "Snapping Andy" - "Hickey" episode, another group of Florence notables arrived in Placerville. Among the number was Bill Mayfield, "Cherokee Bob's" former companion. Mayfield had killed Sheriff Blackburn in Nevada, was captured, tried, and sentenced to be hanged, but made his escape. Coming to Lewiston he joined Plummer, and became prominent among the robbers who pillaged the northern mining camps. Soon after his arrival at Placerville he became involved in a quarrel over a card game with a man named Evans. Mayfield drew his revolver, intending to settle the dispute by killing his adversary, but Evans exclaimed, "I'm not heeled."

"Then go and arm yourself," said Mayfield, replacing his revolver in its holster at his belt; "and look out the next time you meet me, for I am going to kill you at sight. One of us must die."

The next day Mayfield, with a friend, was walking down Granite Street. Evans, in a cabin on the north side of the street, doubtless waiting for Mayfield to appear, fired through a window, using a double-barreled shotgun charged with buckshot. Mayfield, being accustomed to the use of a revolver, even in the act of falling reached for his weapon, but the vital spark had flown. His gun plays were over. He fell in the street, and expired before his friends could remove him; thus illustrating the truth of the maxim, "Those who live by the sword die by it." Evans was placed under arrest, but made his escape the following night, leaving the country on a horse furnished by some friend. He was never apprehended.

But how came this seeming reign of lawlessness to exist at that time? It was not generally known that Congress, in framing and passing the act creating Idaho Territory, had neglected to provide that certain laws should remain in force until other laws were enacted. Idaho was created from parts of four other territories, and Congress could not well provide that the laws of each of the territories infringed upon, in thus creating a new territory, should remain in force. It is presumed that as the easiest way out of their dilemma they passed the enabling act without providing any method of suppressing lawlessness until the Idaho legislature would meet and enact such laws. The act creating Idaho Territory was approved by the President, Abraham Lincoln, March 3, 1863. The first session of the Idaho legislature convened on December 7, of that year. Consequently there were a few days more than nine months, during which Idaho had no penal code, and murder was not defined as a crime.

Startling as this statement may appear, it is extremely doubtful whether during that time laws would have lessened crime greatly. The discoveries of rich placer deposits at Pierce City, Orofino, and Florence had attracted thousands of adventurers from all parts of the United States. Among these were many of as hardened criminals as the world has ever known. The criminal laws and the duly elected sheriffs and constables in near-by territories had little perceptible effect upon these desperate characters, for two years prior to their inclusion in the new Territory of Idaho.

It was not long before we began directly to feel the effects of this lawlessness. My partner, as it chanced, had the first personal contact with it, which also happened to be his first peddling trip. The effect of it was to prejudice him more than ever against the job of peddler.

Porter, you remember, was an Englishman. Although he was born in Canada, he was as thoroughly imbued with the ideas of the English aristocracy as if he had been born and reared in London. One of his national prejudices was to the effect that trade, especially peddling, was a plebeian employment. Consequently, as I had no scruples regarding the method we employed in disposing of the produce of our garden, the task of running the pack animals and peddling our vegetables devolved upon me, while Porter looked after the garden, and kept the "sourdough" can in order.

He did make one trip to Placerville, however, during October, bringing in to me six pack animals loaded with potatoes. In addition to the pack animals he had a saddle horse, making seven animals in all. Discharging his load in Placerville, he started back, driving his animals before him.

He had arrived at the foot of the last hill before the summit. To spare his horse, the hill being very steep, and the trail running zigzag through a dense growth of mountain laurel, he dismounted, and grasping his saddle horse by the tail, started the animals up the trail, following on behind his saddle horse. The animals made the steepest parts of the grade in spurts, and then stopped to take breath.

They were about half the distance to the summit, when three men, two of them masked, arose from the laurel and demanded a halt. At the command the pack animals halted instantly, but Porter did not obey the summons. Dodging behind his saddle horse, and bending as low as possible, he made his way behind the pack animals and escaped over the hill and out to the tollgate, a few hundred yards from where the attempted hold-up occurred. In a short time the pack animals, followed by his saddle horse, came up, and they continued their journey on to the home garden without further adventure or hindrance.

Upon relating this experience with would-be "road agents," Porter insisted that he would recognize the man who wore no mask, if he ever saw him again. I was incredulous, knowing as I did that he could at most have had but a flash view of the man, before dodging behind the horse. He insisted upon his ability to recognize him; and approximately twelve months later he did without any degree of doubt identify the robber.

It afterward transpired that the two men who wore masks were cousins of the one who was maskless, and that they, while having graduated as petty larceny thieves and bogus-dust operators, were novices in the art of highway robbery. The attempt on Porter was probably their first effort in the higher field of illegitimate industry.

"Lowry, dealing Magruder a powerful blow with an
ax, knocked him senseless and killed him."

CHAPTER EIGHT

PIONEER FRIENDSHIP AND JUSTICE

PORTER's adventure was one of common occurrence during
the pioneer days in Idaho, but his escape was the only
incident of like character recorded. The desperate characters who followed highway robbery as a chosen profession were, without exception, out for the money. While
they did not fear, nor care for, the officers of the law, they
had a wholesome respect for the opinions of other desperados, who ridiculed any evidence of tenderness or mercy.

In the summer of 1863, which was the first season of
active industry in the Boisé district, the lawless element
was not so aggressive as during the following year. Then
these outlaws began to prey upon the unsuspecting, either
on the mountain trails, or in the gambling houses. Tragedies which were of frequent occurrence were rarely, if ever,
given to the public. There were no telegraphs or tele-
phones in those days. In all places where men congregated, such subjects as the disappearance of individuals

would ordinarily be discussed, but there were spies who reported daily to their employers, the highwaymen, who promptly made known their disapproval of such discussions.

One circumstance which occurred during the summer of 1863 will cast some light on the character of these desperados, so utterly regardless of human life during that period of the early history of Idaho, which then included Montana. The supplies for the mines at Orofino, Warren, and Florence were shipped during high water, from Portland, Oregon, to Lewiston, Idaho, on river boats. From Lewiston these were forwarded by means of pack trains. New mining camps beyond the Bitter Root Mountains, in the country now included in Montana, were also partly supplied from Lewiston.

The owner of one of these large and well-equipped mule pack trains was a man named Lloyd Magruder. He had been engaged in packing into the Clearwater mines from Lewiston since their discovery, and had acquired and equipped a train of sixty mules. In the spring of 1863, he purchased a cargo of staple goods at Portland and shipped them by boat to Lewiston. His purpose was to pack them into Virginia City, then in Idaho, a distance of about three hundred miles. Magruder had made many warm friends in Lewiston, and in those days of danger friendship was a sacred word. Among these was the proprietor of the principal hotel in that city, a man named Hill Beachy.

Having made so many trips into the mountains without encountering serious difficulty, Magruder appeared to have no apprehension of impending danger. Beachy, the hotel proprietor, was in a position to know the kind of characters his friend was likely to encounter. As a precaution he lent Magruder a reliable gun and warned him to be on his guard. The snow having disappeared from the summit of the Bitter Root Mountains, Magruder made good time. He reached Virginia City without the loss of a single animal or pack.

Soon after crossing the summit he had been joined by a party of mounted men who had one pack horse to carry their blankets and provisions. The party included three men whom Magruder had met in Lewiston — D. C. Lowry, David Howard, and James Romain. As they appeared to be in no hurry, these men traveled along with Magruder the remainder of the distance to Virginia City. And as jolly good fellows, which they seemed to be, they all assisted in loading the cargo every morning. This very materially aided Magruder in his progress with such a large train of mules.

Arriving at Virginia City Magruder erected a large tent and at once began disposing of his cargo. He found a ready market, but before the remnants of such a mixed stock of goods could be disposed of the season had advanced into October. A heavy fall of snow was liable to occur on the Bitter Root Mountains at any time after the middle of that month, so Magruder decided to return home without further delay.

He hastily employed the first men he could engage. The three men whose acquaintance he had made on the trail, whom he had no reason to suspect, expressed a willingness to return with him, as did also one of the original party, William Page, a trapper. Taking these four men, Magruder hired two others, a man named Philips and another named Allen. Two more young men, trying to return to their homes in Missouri, also joined the party. Each of these had secured about two thousand dollars in gold dust. If they gave their names to Magruder before starting he probably made an entry in his diary, which was destroyed, consequently their names were never made known.

The start on the return trip was made under very favorable circumstances. The mules after so long a rest were in good condition, and everything appeared to bespeak a speedy and pleasant trip. Such it proved to be until more than half the distance to Lewiston was covered. Then one night, while the party was camped on the Bitter Root Mountains the carefully laid tragedy was enacted. As nearly as can be determined by the evidence obtained, it had been planned by Lowry, Howard, and Romain before leaving Lewiston, to rob Magruder. It seems probable that their first plan was to murder him and his packers while on their way to Virginia City, and appropriate the mules and cargo; but as they could not assemble enough of their gang successfully to carry out that enterprise, it was safer to permit Magruder to sell his goods, and take the proceeds while he was on the trail to Lewiston. The entire party were to be killed, except Page, the trapper.

A night was chosen when Magruder and his party had camped on a ridge which broke off on one side, almost perpendicular for several hundred feet, into a cañon or mountain gorge. Near the summit was a spring which furnished the camp with water. From a confession made by Page, the trapper, it was revealed that on the night selected for the massacre, Page was placed on guard and told what was going to happen. He was ordered to keep still under penalty of death. Magruder and Lowry were also on guard in an opposite direction from Page, while Allen and the other men were asleep in their blankets near the fire.

During the first watch of the night, Lowry approached within striking distance, and dealing Magruder a powerful blow with an ax which he had concealed under his coat, knocked him senseless and killed him. The sleeping men in camp were also speedily dispatched. Page, the trapper, who was watching the mules near by, and afterwards turned state's evidence, claimed that he saw the murders committed.

As soon as daylight arrived the mules were driven in and five of the best were selected. Four of these were used for saddle animals and one to pack the murderers' camp outfit and plunder. The other animals were then driven into a deep cañon and they too were killed. The murdered men were tied in blankets and dropped over the bluff near camp, into the bottom of the cañon several hundred feet below. After this, having secured the gold dust, they made a bonfire and burned all the camp equipment.

This done, they started for the lower country. They expected to ford the Clearwater above Lewiston and keep on down the north bank, thus avoiding the town. But when they reached the river, the weather having turned cold, the water was full of running ice, so they were afraid to attempt to ford. Going into camp they remained there until the following night, when they quietly entered Lewiston.

They found a stock ranchman with whom they left their mules, and took the early morning stage for Walla Walla. In those days passengers from Lewiston to Portland, Oregon, took passage first on the stage to Walla Walla, then on a second stage line from Walla Walla to Wallula. From that point passage was secured by steamer, including two portages, to Portland.

Hill Beachy, the proprietor of the hotel at Lewiston, upon learning that four men had entered town in the night disguised, and taken the early stage out in the morning, became suspicious. Intuitively he seemed to surmise that the travelers had robbed Magruder. So strong was this intuition that he made complaint before an officer. As the Governor of Idaho chanced to be in Lewiston at the time, he obtained requisitions on the governors of Oregon, Washington, and California.

Beachy intended to start immediately in pursuit, prepared to have the murderers extradited, no matter in which of the foregoing states they might be found. His friends, however, persuaded him to wait a few days to see if some evidence could not be found. Learning that the men whom he suspected had left mules to be sent out to a ranch, he had the animals and saddles sent in for inspection. One of the mules was recognized at once as Magruder's saddle animal, and one of the saddles as formerly belonging to Magruder. This evidence removed the last lingering doubt.

Beachy then started in pursuit of the murderers, engaging a man named Pike to accompany him. He took a private conveyance, and changing horses several times, they made a rapid drive to Walla Walla. Thence they took the stage to Wallula, from which point they took passage by steamer to Portland. There they learned that four men answering the description of those wanted had been in the city a few days previous, and while there seemed to be well provided with money. In fact, they had made a deposit in a faro bank of several hundred dollars. But they had departed on a steamship bound for San Francisco.

Beachy sent Pike after them by water route, while he started overland. He did not care to await the next steamer, for at that time the sailing days were infrequent. The overland trip from Portland, Oregon, to Sacramento, California, by stage was one that few men cared to undertake. The roads up the Willamette and Umpqua valleys were proverbial for sticky mud and deep chuck holes. Since the stages ran both night and day the passengers had little opportunity for rest or sleep. Yet without hesitancy

Beachy boarded the Concord Coach, and started overland, fixed in his determination to capture the murderers of his friend.

After three days and nights cooped up in the stage, he reached Yreka. This was then the nearest point from Portland where telegraphic communication could be had with San Francisco. From here he telegraphed a full description of the suspects to the chief of police in San Francisco, giving a brief account of the murder and requesting that the men described be arrested and held. The request was carried out. Upon his arrival a few days later, he found the men behind prison bars. In addition to the arrest, the police had traced to the United States Mint the gold dust the men had brought with them on the steamer.

After some delay, during which Tom Pike arrived, Beachy, with his prisoners securely ironed, took the steamer for Portland and thence proceeded to Lewiston. They arrived there on the 7th of December, 1863. This was the same day on which convened the first session of the legislative assembly of the Territory of Idaho. Before leaving San Francisco, William Page, the trapper, confessed to Beachy the particulars of the tragedy.

Had Beachy been a man of less determination, the citizens would undoubtedly have given the four prisoners but short shrift. He told the enraged people, however, that the prisoners were his, and that before leaving San Francisco, he had promised them that they should have a fair trial by jury. His promise must and would be kept.

The first district court to be held in Idaho Territory was to be convened on January 5, 1864, about one month from the first day of the legislative session. The four men then in custody, charged with the atrocious murder of Magruder and his party, were to be tried during that term of court, though as yet Idaho had no Criminal Practice Act.

However, the members of the first legislature were equal to the occasion. They promptly passed

An Act Adopting the Common Law of England:

Be it Enacted by the Legislative Assembly of the Territory of Idaho, as follows:

Section 1: The common law of England, so far as the same is not inconsistent with the provisions of the Constitution of the United States, the Organic Act and laws of this territory, shall be the law of the land in this territory.

Section 2: This act to take effect and be in force from and after its approval by the governor.

The act was approved January 4, 1864.

Thus one day in advance of the coming trial the district court was provided with authority to cover any void existing heretofore in the statute. Judge Samuel C. Parks was assigned to hold the first term of district court in Lewiston, beginning on the 5th day of January, 1864. Of the four men held for the murder of the Magruder party, Lowry, Howard, and Romain were indicted for murder in the first degree. They were placed on trial at once, and promptly convicted, as the chain of evidence was complete.

William Page, the trapper, having turned state's evidence, was permitted to depart after the trial. Rumor has it that he was killed soon after, but by whom is not definitely known. The three convicted men were sentenced by Judge Parks, on January 26, to be hanged on March 4, 1864, by the neck until dead. The execution of this trio of human fiends struck terror to the hearts of their kind, and caused a prompt reinforcing of the troop of scoundrels who had already transferred their activities to Boisé Basin and other congenial camps.

The territorial legislature being in session during the

progress of the trial of the murderers, upon the recommendation of Judge Parks made an appropriation to pay Hill Beachy for the pursuit and capture of the Magruder murderers, including expenses thereto, $6244.00. The money found on the prisoners, together with what they had deposited in the United States Mint at San Francisco, was paid to the family of Magruder. The loyalty of Hill Beachy to his friend, combined with his native fearlessness and determination thus brought the episode to a successful ending.

The following spring Hill Beachy, with a party of six others, visited the scene of the tragedy and buried the remains of the victims. The particulars of the gruesome find, and the details of their trip, after being written and signed by all the party, were printed in a Lewiston paper. This removed every doubt as to the testimony of Page, upon whose evidence the men were convicted.

Taken all in all the tragic episode is a clear example of pioneer justice. The officers of the law, including the members of the legislature, filled promptly the need of laws to meet the situation, which Congress had failed to provide. The court brought about speedy but dignified action, and a just penalty was quickly imposed.

" They indicated that they desired to have a talk."

CHAPTER NINE

PROSPECTORS AND PIUTES

DURING the summer of 1862, a party of prospectors entered the Boisé Basin. The party had come by way of Boisé Valley, near the point where now stands the hamlet of Centerville. It was there that one of their number made the first discovery of gold in that subsequently famous district. The discovery was made in the gravel of a small stream afterwards named Grimes Creek, for a member of the party. Moving from there up the creek a few miles, they made a second camp, where they remained two days, prospecting the stream and adjacent gravel bars.

While coming in from Boisé Valley they met a party of Indians. One of the redmen, who could speak some English, informed them that there were "plenty bad Indians" in the mountains where they were going. After crossing the divide and dropping down into the Basin the prospectors found several Indian tepees, but up to the time of making their last camp on Grimes Creek the party had not been

81

molested.   One day, however, an attack was made, and Grimes was shot and killed while charging upon a group of Indians, concealed in a thicket of bushes.   Fortunately the rest of the men rallied to their leader, a man named Splawn, and repulsed the Indians without further loss.

The prospectors realized that they were in a dangerous position.   They were few in number, in a hostile country, remote from reinforcements or any base of supplies.   Their provisions and ammunition, too, were running low.   Their only hope seemed to be in retreat.   Assembled around the lifeless body of their late companion, they held a council. It was determined that after Grimes had been decently buried, they would start at once for Walla Walla, carrying the news of their discovery and a sample of the gold dust they had obtained.

Wrapped in a blanket, the body of Grimes was tenderly laid to rest in one of the recently dug prospect holes.   Thus was left under the whispering pines one of the brave pioneers.   Having endured the hardships incident to frontier life, he had finally answered to the last call with breast to foe.   It was a simple but impressive service.   Those who have been accustomed to witness burial ceremonies in long-established communities, have listened to the solemn invocation of the chaplain, and admired the banks of flowers placed by loving friends upon the casket, can have but a faint conception of the details of such a tragic burial as was conducted by those grim-visaged men.   Every one of them knew that even before their task was completed rifle shots might summon others of their little party to a similar obsequies ; yet those brave men gave their fallen companion and friend a Christian burial, before they departed and left him alone in the wilderness.   It was by men of such mettle that the trails were blazed to the gold mines in Idaho.

Placer gold was first found in Boisé Basin in August, 1862. The discoverers, after many vicissitudes, arrived at Walla Walla in September. A return party was immediately organized, and before the inclemency of winter impeded travel, many hundreds of miners had reached the new field of mining adventure, and most of these had succeeded in locating claims and erected cabins. Hundreds of pack animals had also arrived laden with provisions and other supplies. These were soon distributed among the several mining towns, which had sprung up like magic.

The Indians who attacked the prospecting party and killed Grimes were doubtless in the mountains at that time for the purpose of gathering pine nuts. As their stay in the higher altitudes is generally brief, it is probable that they fled to where the tribe had its winter quarters, in southeastern Oregon, immediately after their attack upon the Grimes party. This conclusion is borne out by the fact that no Indians were seen in the Boisé Basin at any time subsequently.

In the spring of 1863, raiding parties of Piutes made occasional forays across Snake River into the lower valleys of Boisé and Payette. They took back with them bands of horses and mules, as well as the scalps of their owners. This species of warfare, however, was not long endured by the hardy and venturesome men who had wintered in that country, and were familiar with the story of Grimes' murder by this same tribe of Indians.

A company of volunteers was soon enrolled in the Basin. Under the leadership of Jeff Standifer, these Indian fighters marched down the Payette Valley, crossing Snake River at the Washoe ferry, and made straight for the camp of the Indians who had raided lower Boisé Valley. The volunteers located the enemy in a very strong position. The band of Indians could be approached only over open ground, occupying as they did a rocky elevation which afforded ample cover from gunfire. Had the company been regular soldiers, it is probable that their officers would have ordered a charge. The men who followed Standifer, however, were not disciplined to that style of tactics.

They camped beyond reach of the Indians' rifles, and proceeded to experiment on a means by which they could approach the stronghold without exposing themselves to certain annihilation. First they constructed a framework of light poles, filling the center with grass. It was so light that two or three men could carry it in advance while approaching the Indians. Before putting this shield to actual use it was thought best to try it out and see whether it would resist gunfire. Alas! it was discovered that the portable shield would afford no protection; a bullet fired from any gun in the party would penetrate it like so much paper.

They next hit upon the plan of cutting and assembling basket willows into large bundles. These they found could be rolled by two men sheltered behind such a bundle. Upon trial it was also found that willows bound in bundles about the size of a barrel would resist a bullet.

The Indians were watching the experiments made by Standifer and his men. When they saw that the bundles of willows could be rolled by men sheltered behind them, and thus their camp could be reached with but little danger to the attacking party, they displayed a flag of truce. They indicated that they desired to have a talk, and hold a council.

Under the white flag Standifer and his men gained entrance to the Indians' stronghold. But once inside, they failed to respect the universal emblem of amity, and at once proceeded to massacre the Indians — men, women, and children. Of the entire number of Indians only three escaped; two boys, one of whom was probably ten or twelve years old and the other no more than five or six, and a young woman of perhaps twenty years.

Standifer brought the captives back with him, and gave them to such persons as would receive them. A man named Ira Worden and his wife, who kept a restaurant in Centerville, took the woman and gave her a home. The younger of the boys was adopted by the then-famous violinist, John Kelly, a big-hearted Irishman. Eventually Kelly became as strongly attached to the boy as if he had been his own son. The boy developed wonderful musical talent under the violinist's training. The elder of the boys was given to me.

I expected to teach him to be useful in the garden and in handling the pack train; but he proved to be sullen. Although I had another Indian boy of about his age, he would not attempt to talk to him or any of my men. Eventually I succeeded in inducing an Englishman who was engaged in freighting to take the boy with him on the road. Some months later I learned that the Englishman sold the boy to a railroad contractor for one hundred dollars. The contractor wanted the boy for a house servant, and gave him a good home, his wife being a humane and Christian woman.

It would be an injustice to the early pioneers of the Boisé Basin to pass over the incident of the massacre of the Indians on the Malheur, without stating that Standifer and his men were not representative citizens of the district from which they came. They were of the "bravo" type, who held that "the only good Indian is a dead one." Their action was deplored by every manly man who learned of the tragedy.

The sadness of it all comes with the thought that the occupation by the whites of the best grazing grounds brought hunger to many a tepee, to Indian wives and children. Is it to be wondered at that the brigandage we practiced was resented in the only manner they recognized — an appeal to arms? In their efforts to conquer the wilderness many pioneers lost their lives, many homes were made desolate; but upon the ashes of these and similar tragedies has arisen not only the commonwealth of Idaho, but also the United States of America. Our only justification lies in the assertion that "the march of progress means a survival of the fittest."

"A few seconds served to usher every able-bodied man on to the street."

CHAPTER TEN

A MINING BATTLE UPSET BY INDIAN TROUBLES

ONE foray against the Indians in which as a volunteer I took part, gave us a touch of real excitement for a few days, breaking up temporarily a tense legal battle over a fabulously rich mining claim, and bringing the disputants into one band bent on the common purpose of clearing the region of redskin raiders. This brief but stirring campaign was the direct result not of Indian depredations, but of the work of a band of horse thieves operating in the vicinity of the mining camps.

These reprobates deliberately planned to have the Indians blamed for all losses of stock. For that purpose they carried with them bows and arrows, moccasins, and other paraphernalia common to Indians. When running off stock, the thieves would often shoot an arrow into some animal which was lagging behind and then drive the others on, leaving the wounded horse or mule, with perhaps an

Indian saddle, and plenty of moccasin tracks, to misinform their pursuers.

The owners of the stolen stock would almost invariably appeal to the keepers of the nearest roadhouse for volunteers to help recover their stock. They had no thought that white men, not Indians, were the actual raiders, so it often happened that the very men to whom they appealed for help were interested in the success of the raid, being members of the thieves' organization. It was a piece of deviltry of this sort that touched off the campaign just suggested, and brought about in time a clearing up of the whole situation.

Some immigrants who had lost their animals turned at once to a certain roadhouse for help. The keepers of the roadhouse appeared shocked. Immediately they expressed their willingness to help capture the Indians, and appointed one of their number to join in the pursuit, one man, they said, being all that could be spared from the roadhouse station. But to show their sympathy and good faith, they proffered to furnish saddle animals and equipment for the owners. Accompanied by their volunteer companion, the owners struck out after the fleeing robbers.

After a pursuit of several hours, the trail entered a narrow gorge in the lava formation. As they went into the defile, several rifle shots rang out, and at once the air was rent by the blood-curdling war whoop of what appeared to be a band of Indians, whose war bonnets were discernible among the rocks. Although the owners were anxious to recover their stock, they were more anxious to save their lives. Whirling their saddle animals, they made a hasty retreat, out of range of the hostile guns. Without halting they continued their flight to Burnt River, where they spread the news of their disaster and repulse by the Indians.

The account of this fiasco, together with several similar occurrences during the seasons named, were heralded far and wide. They served to confirm the belief that the Indians owned vast herds of valuable animals. Eventually this belief led to the organization of a company of adventurers, consisting of forty men, whose object was to enter the Indian country south and west of the Owyhee mining towns and give battle to the Indians, whom they expected to find scattered in small parties or bands at that season of the year. By attacking them in detached parties they hoped to recover the stolen stock without serious resistance.

The men in this company were all in the vigor of early manhood; many of them of the type who swagger around mining towns and pose as "gunmen." Their leader, Jennings, who was somewhat older, was a man of character, an experienced mountaineer and Indian trailer and fighter. The men were all accustomed to outdoor life, well mounted, supplied with pack animals to carry their camp equipage, including provisions for a three months' campaign, and armed with the most effective and modern firearms procurable at that time.

As the company crossed Snake River and began its march into the trackless country west of the Owyhee mountains, it was remarked by the bystanders that no more formidable troop had ever started in pursuit of Indians, in any country. This expression was indorsed by all present, and it was generally predicted that at last the Piutes would be taught a well-deserved lesson. Defeat of the company was considered impossible, by any force the Indians could bring against them.

The district court convened in Ruby City during the second week of the absence of the Indian fighters. A famous case, that of the "Poor Man" mining claim, being on trial, the town was full of court officers, witnesses, experts, and partisans of the rival companies. The contest had grown out of the discovery of a chimney of valuable ore made by two prospectors who were wandering around over War Eagle Mountain, in search of precious metal. By chance one of them struck his pick into a fabulously rich vein of ore. The discovery happened to be on the line of the property of a certain mining company; but the prospectors, associating with themselves a capitalist willing to take the risk of the venture along with them, then went ahead digging out the ore, richly laden, not only with silver but with gold. They worked their men by night and succeeded before the contest for the property was launched in getting approximately $250,000 worth of ore from their find.

Then an injunction was filed against them as trespassers. The court sustained the writ, giving the contending parties ninety days during which they were to prosecute development work on their respective claims within a given number of feet of the disputed ore. They were then to come into court and show by comparison of the ore, to which lode the ore in dispute probably belonged. During the ninety days, while the decision was pending, the respective companies erected miniature fortresses overlooking the disputed ground. These they garrisoned with various reputed "gunmen," whose revolvers were decorated with sundry notches as evidence of former activities.

When court convened at Ruby City, and the Poor Man case was called for trial, intense excitement prevailed. The United States Marshal's office was represented by numerous deputies prepared to enforce the orders of the court, and a company of United States Infantry was encamped at Boonville, a few miles distant from Ruby City. Whether the soldiers had come on their annual practice march, or in accordance with a request of the Governor of Idaho Territory, that they might be at hand to help suppress any riot that might occur, only the officers knew. As the trial progressed, various rumors fanned the excitement. One rumor was rife that the men who discovered the Poor Man, with their associates, did not propose to submit to the decision of the court unless in their favor, because, as another rumor had it, the Judge had been bribed by the adverse party. These rumors, which could not be traced to any reliable origin, kept things at fever pitch.

The officers and the general public, the wearied citizens, — those who were not "night hawks" — retired one night for a much-needed rest; but they were not permitted to enjoy their usual morning nap. The first rays of the morning sun had just appeared on War Eagle Mountain, when the sleepers were started from their dreams by the steam whistles of the Quartz Mills, and the gongs of the hotels and restaurants. The first thought of almost every person was that the Indians had attacked the town. Then there was hurrying to and fro, in search of boots, trousers, and arms. A few seconds, not minutes, served to usher every able-bodied man on to the street, ready to follow the current of humanity which immediately started toward a meeting place in front of a popular saloon.

Arrived there, the men were called to order by a prominent merchant. He stated that our company of volunteers who had gone into the Indian country some weeks before had been attacked, and surrounded by a large force of Indians, estimated to be five hundred warriors. The volunteers had retreated from the point of attack to where they had camped the night previous, and there had thrown up rifle pits in the lava rocks, and were holding the Indians off.

There was no chance for the men to retreat. They had

been fighting already two days when the scouts who had arrived crawled through the Indian lines, and made their way to the settlements. These scouts had traveled the first night, and concealed themselves during the following day. Without water they had finished their long tramp, estimated to be sixty miles, and just arrived with the news. A rescue must be made soon, or not a man would remain to tell the tale of their annihilation.

The mining camp trouble was swept aside by the whirl-wind of excitement that followed. A call was immediately made for volunteers, and while men were being enrolled, Judge Kelly appeared and announced that when he convened court that morning, he would at once adjourn for ten days. This action was taken to permit lawyers and others to enlist for the rescue of the men held by the Indians.

There were no laggards present that morning. The question resolved itself into one of animals to ride, rather than men. Every one present was anxious to join the rescuing company. Finally, by confiscating freight teams and pack trains, about a hundred riding animals were secured. Evidently not all who volunteered could be mounted; some must be left behind.

Those who were selected and mounted moved on, without organization, to the little mining camp of Flint. There a halt was made and the men divided themselves into three companies. Each company then elected a captain, who was authorized to appoint one lieutenant. There was no contest for position in the company in which I had taken a place; I was chosen unanimously as captain.

The alarm had been given, and the call for volunteers had been made before the breakfast hour. During the excitement which ensued, but few, if any of the men who volunteered were provident enough to obtain even a cup of coffee before starting on the trail. We were assured, however, that an express would immediately follow us with provisions sufficient to last until we reached the beleaguered men. None of us appeared to realize that the express might fail to overtake our troop; which proved to be the result. It was a set of hungry men who started out of Flint on their march to the rescue.

The guides who had arrived with the news of the dilemma having been provided with saddle animals, took the lead, and directed our course. We marched the first day, making only one halt to allow our stock to graze, and to take a short rest. From the information the guides gave us as to distance and route, we confidently expected to cover the distance and attack the Indians before sunrise the following morning, provided we traveled all night. Unfortunately our guides became bewildered during the night, and missing their way led us into a volcanic gorge, from which we had difficulty in extricating our saddle animals, and in so doing lost much time.

Daylight found us once more on the move; but our guides appeared uncertain as to the direction in which we would find the men and Indians. The region being of lava formation, presented such a uniform appearance of desolation that their task as guides was very difficult. However, we continued on until late in the forenoon of the second day we came to water in a little meadow where there was an abundance of grass for our jaded animals. There we halted and gave our guides an opportunity to determine the location of the party we desired to relieve.

After an interval of an hour they returned and reported that we were then within a few miles of the oasis where they had left the men; but there being no sound of firing, it might be that the Indians had already captured the men and moved on. In any event we should proceed with caution, and if the Indians were still there they advised that we move up without display, until we arrived at a certain point of rocks, where we were to deploy and charge the Indians, to bring on an engagement at close quarters, so that revolvers, with which every man was armed, might be more effective. The prearranged plan was carried out, but when we entered the position the Indians had held during their effort to dislodge the volunteers, we found it deserted. The Piutes, who had probably discovered the dust of our approach, had retreated, rather than give battle to an unknown force.

"They had progressed without adventure or accident until the foremost company was approaching the Owyhee River."

CHAPTER ELEVEN

THE STORY OF THE SIEGE

OUR arrival was opportune. The ammunition of the beleaguered men was nearly exhausted. However, they were still well supplied with provisions, consequently they were able to supply the wants of their hungry reinforcements. While we were fed, we were given the particulars of their adventures since starting out to hunt Indians. From the narrative we learned that while it is rare sport to hunt Indians, it is entirely the reverse when the Indians turn the tables and become the pursuers instead of being the pursued.

During the time they were in the field they had succeeded in cutting off two small raiding parties of Indians and capturing their stock. These proved to be ponies, such as the Indians usually own; they did not have any mules or American horses. The volunteer company finally came upon a trail which had been recently traveled by a large party of Indians — men, women, and children.

Following it, they found that the Indians had camped at the same watering place where the recent battle had culminated. As it was late in the afternoon when they made this discovery, they too camped in the same place. Next morning they took the Indians' trail in pursuit. It proved to be but two or three miles from their recent camping ground to a crossing of the Owyhee River.

In that region the river runs in a deep gorge or cut in the volcanic rock. There are but few places where an animal, or even a man, can descend the walls from the plateau above to the river below; and after such descent is made, the opportunities are rare where it is possible to climb out on the opposite side of the river.

The ford and crossing to which the Indian trail led was one of the few where the river could be approached from both sides. When the pursuing party arrived at the bluff from which the trail descended to the water, and from which it could be plainly seen that the main body of the Indians had crossed to the other side, some one in the troop or party suggested the propriety of precaution in attempting a crossing, as those lava rocks might conceal a party of Indians.

One of the men exclaimed, "Oh, I'll bet that we don't see another Indian on the trip!" Spurring his horse down the trail, he was joined by two others who also desired to display their bravery.

The main body of the men, however, remained upon the bluff. One of their number, who possessed a pair of small opera glasses, carefully scrutinized the opposite rocks, until he finally saw an Indian skulk from one hiding place to another. He gave the alarm, and the men who had already reached the river and were fording it, wheeled their horses and turned back. The Indians who were concealed in the rocks, realizing that their

ambuscade was discovered, fired at them; but the fool-
hardy riders escaped safely to their comrades on the
bluff, wiser if not better men.

"The Indians confined their assault to a fusillade, at long
range, on the rear."

The company had with them two trappers who acted as
scouts, both of whom spoke the Piute language. Under
instruction they challenged the Indians to come over
and fight; but the Indians were not required to cross
back over the river. There were plenty of other Indians
concealed among the rocks on the same side near the
whites. A band of mounted Indians, estimated to number
seventy warriors, rode out of a ravine a short distance
above, and circled around the volunteers, discharging
their guns as they galloped by. From the beginning of
their attack, however, they showed sufficient respect
for the white men's firearms to keep out of their range.

This first display of force by the Indians was evidence
enough to the men that their only hope for their lives was
to retreat to the camp ground they had occupied the
previous night. Accordingly, without delay, the retreat
began. Fortunately the intervening ground between
the river and their objective was an open plateau, and
the Indians did not attempt to check the progress of

their intended victims by an attack on their front, but confined their assault to a fusillade, at long range, on the rear.

No more masterly retreat of a company of men, under attack by a superior force, was ever made in any country. The horses were bunched well to the front of the column, while a few of the best marksmen dismounted, protected the rear, and kept the Indians back by a well-directed fire. The details of that retreat, which was made in a most orderly manner, slowly as was necessary, and with the rear guard as footmen, would be fascinating literature to those interested in military tactics. Marvellous as it will always appear, those men arrived at, and immediately took possession of, their former camp, without the loss of a man or horse.

During my residence of more than half a century in Idaho, I never have discovered another camp ground so well adapted to defense by a small party of men. It was an oasis in the volcanic rock containing two springs of pure water, each of which was surrounded and partly concealed by a dense growth of large willows. These willow thickets were but a few rods apart, and were situated in what appeared to be a settling down in the rock formation. The rim rock which surrounded these springs rose to a greater elevation than the ground immediately in its rear, consequently to protect the springs it was only necessary to erect rifle pits on the rim rock above the willows.

Upon the arrival of the men, closely pursued as they were by an overwhelming force of Indians, they at once posted men on the rim. These began to gather loose rock, with which the rim was covered, and erect shelter from the fire of the Indians. Meanwhile, the hostiles were held back while the saddle and pack animals were secured by crowding them into the larger clump of willows. The smaller clump was economized as a storehouse for the provisions, and a shelter for the cook, whose culinary efforts were confined, principally, to providing coffee for the men, during the nighttime, when the danger of exposure to Indian rifle practice was reduced to the minimum.

The first night after taking possession of the rim rock, Jennings and several of his men succeeded in gathering enough loose rock to build a wall four feet high around an area sufficient to shelter one-half of his company, and permit them to lie down and take necessary rest. This was to be the main station from which the sentinels at other posts were to be relieved. While work on the main station was in progress three other stations were completed. All were built of lava rock such as was strewn over the ridges, each being designed to shelter two or more men while sitting down or occupying a recumbent position.

When morning dawned, and the Indians saw what the white men had accomplished during the night, they immediately opened fire all along their lines, directing special attention to an effort to kill or wound the animals, which were secured in the thicket of willows; but most of their shots fell short. During the first day, however, they succeeded in killing two horses, which during the following night were removed by dragging them down the water course to a sufficient distance to avoid the stench of decaying flesh.

The whites realized from the time their first stand was made that their situation was hopeless, unless they were reinforced. As their location was distant from any traveled road or trail, it was unlikely that word of their predicament would reach the settlement until too late for their rescue. Their only chance therefore hinged upon the possibility of one or two of their number escaping through the Indian outposts, and making their way, without detection, to Silver and Ruby cities, in time to bring reinforcements in sufficient numbers to overpower the Indians.

The two trappers or scouts who had accompanied the party volunteered for the attempt. Although it was a bright, starlight night, shod with moccasins constructed out of gunny sacks, they crawled over the ridge, and passed by the Indian outposts without detection. After a wearisome march, these heroes reached Ruby City, to meet an eager welcome and response to their appeal for aid.

During their absence the Indians had continued the siege, giving the men but little rest, or opportunity to eat. In consequence of a scarcity of fuel, it was a difficult task for the Dutch cook to prepare food. Upon our arrival we found that the ammunition for their guns was nearly exhausted. They were almost entirely dependent upon their revolvers to repulse an assault, should the Indians muster courage to charge upon their barricades. Only one of the party had been killed during the siege, and only one wounded.

The man killed was known as Caton, and he had given his residence when enrolled as Long Tom, Oregon. He was the only man in the company who had made a record of their daily activities and adventures. He had kept a diary, in which he had recorded, each day, events as they transpired, all of which were written in a scholarly manner, in a neat and legible hand.

A small rifle pit had been constructed approximately two hundred yards north of the main station, at a point where loose rock was scarce. The wall they erected around it was so low that the two men who usually garrisoned it obtained shelter only by lying flat upon the

"Caton raised his head to investigate."

ground. Caton and a companion had been detailed to relieve the occupants of that station. Soon after the change was effected, and while Caton, lying on his stomach, was engaged in writing up his diary, his attention was probably attracted by the snapping of a twig, or some other suspicious noise, which he raised his head to investigate. An Indian who had wormed his way within effective distance, took deadly aim and shot him in the forehead. He dropped back with his diary beside him, the sentence he was writing when startled punctuated by his lifeblood.

His comrade remained with his dead body until darkness made it possible for him to return to the main station with the sad news. Caton's remains were permitted to lie where he fell until the next night, when a detail of his former comrades was dispatched to bring in his body for burial. They found him undisturbed. The Indians had not even removed his gun. His burial had occurred before the arrival of our relieving party, and one of his comrades pointed out to me the little sodless mound which marked the final resting place of his friend, and with lowered voice he related incidents of Caton's kindness and bravery.

The man who was wounded was hit by a partly spent rifle bullet, which took effect in his hip. It lodged against the joint, without shattering the bone, but produced a very painful wound. Some kind of litter must be improvised to carry him back to where he could receive surgical treatment, as it was impossible for him to stand on that limb or even to sit in a saddle.

As mentioned before, a company of United States Infantry was camped near Ruby City. When the call came for men to relieve the beleaguered volunteers, it was not thought to be worth while to notify the captain in command, as the distance to the beleaguered men was too great for infantry to march. However, the alarm was soon spread to Boonville, and the Captain, learning of the possible need of more help than had been sent, ordered in his train of pack animals, and lashing blankets on them in the absence of saddles, mounted his men and was soon on his way to the scene of action, following the trail we had made. Although handicapped by want of saddles for his men, he came near overtaking us. Within half an hour after our arrival, he brought his troop to a salute, alongside the principal station. It is needless to say that seldom, if ever, in Idaho at that time was a company of United States troops received with a more ringing cheer.

The day following our arrival was devoted to giving our horses a rest, and making preparation for the return of such lawyers and court officials as were expected to return to their posts of duty before the expiration of the ten days' adjournment. It was evident that the Indians were well supplied with ammunition. They had been able to maintain during the siege an almost continuous fusillade. They had also a better store of rations than the meager supply which usually constituted the commissary of the Piute Indians. During the day we remained upon the scene of battle, some of our men, in search of souvenirs, came upon the place to which the Indians carried their wounded, and where they had given them primitive first-aid treatment. The ground in this immediate locality was strewn with wads of blood-stained cotton which had evidently been used to stanch the blood of the wounded warriors.

This discovery made clear the source of the Indians' plentiful supply of ammunition and rations. A few weeks previous two companies of Chinamen on their way from California to the placer mines in Idaho were traveling over what was known as the "Chico route." They had several wagons loaded with provisions and other supplies common to the needs of Chinamen. They had progressed without adventure or accident until the foremost company was approaching the crossing of the Owyhee River. Without warning, and with blood-curdling yells, hundreds of Indians arose in the sagebrush on both sides of the road. They began firing upon the Orientals who, abandoning their wagons and teams, attempted to escape by seeking shelter in the sagebrush which was unusually tall at that point. It was related by a party of prospectors who witnessed the attack from a range of hills within view of the tragedy, that the Indians chased the Orientals around in the brush for hours, and but few escaped. The capture of the Chinamen's plunder accounted for the blood-stained cotton. It had been taken from the wadding of the shirts or coats commonly worn by Orientals. The general supplies captured with the trains provided ample ammunition and rations to enable the Piutes to prolong the siege until the white men had exhausted their supply. As the besieged party did not know whether their scouts had safely escaped through the Indian lines with news of their desperate dilemma, the prospect before the relief appeared was very gloomy. The Indians, believing that escape through their lines was impossible, were confident of eventually securing the white men's scalps, together with their arms and horses. There was one Indian in the attacking party who evidently had lived at an army post or Indian agency, for he appeared to delight in displaying his ability to speak English. It was his daily custom to call over to the whites and ask derisively, "When you go?" "Where your soldiers?" Victory, the Indians felt, was only a question of a short time.

The second morning after our arrival at the battle ground the men divided into two groups. The original forty, now reduced to thirty-eight, proposed to follow the Indians, and a considerable number of the rescuing party joined them. The members of my company, and several of the men belonging to the other companies, decided to return to Silver or Ruby Cities. Accordingly we started soon after daylight, carrying with us the wounded man. On his account our progress was slow ; but on the evening of the third day we arrived safely at our destination. The wounded man endured the journey bravely, and without apparent irritation of his wound.

The news of our return spread quickly. In a short time a crowd had assembled in front of the hotel where we had carried our patient. Surgeons were quickly summoned, and after a hasty examination they pronounced that while the wound was not apt to prove fatal, it would probably be weeks, if not months, before the young man would recover sufficiently to be able to work. When this announcement became known, a committee was immediately appointed to solicit contributions to carry the young man back to his home in one of the Middle-Western states. A few minutes sufficed to raise a subscription of seven hundred dollars. A greater amount might have been raised had small contributions been received. The big-hearted men who worked in the mines and mills were all clamorous to contribute their mite, but it was considered more appropriate for the mine owners, many of whom were millionaires, to advance the money, especially as during our absence the litigants in the Poor Man case had come to an amicable settlement of their respective claims, and the service of highly paid "gunmen" was no longer required.

Two weeks later part of the men who had continued their pursuit of the Indians returned, and reported that they had failed to overtake them. The pursuing party, having quarreled among themselves, divided into small detachments, each pursuing separate ways. But one object was gained by these scouting parties: they finally settled the question whether the Indians had stolen the stock on Burnt River. The public was convinced that the contrary was the truth; the Indians had no such stolen stock.

"Major Lugenbeil arrived with a company of United States cavalry-men."

CHAPTER TWELVE

THE FOUNDING OF BOISÉ

THE Indian and other troubles stimulated the forwarding of numerous requests to Washington for the establishment of a military post in Boisé Valley. The settlers wanted protection not only from the Indians, but from a truly more dangerous class of savages, the lawless whites. In accordance with such requests, Major Lugenbeil, on June 28, 1863, had arrived with a company of United States cavalrymen. He went into camp on what had since been known as "Government Island," a mile or more down the river from where Boisé now stands, and on the 6th day of July, the same year, selected the present site of Boisé Barracks.

A few days later a number of men from Bannock, now Idaho City, came down and located the town site of Boisé, the present capital of Idaho. Little time was required to make of the new town a busy mart. A cargo of goods owned by Cyrus Jacobs, which was then in transit to Bannock, was diverted to the embryo city of Boisé, and a store was speedily erected. Another stock of goods was soon shipped in by Crawford and Slocum, who established another store. Several saloons, two livery stables, and two hotels were rapidly placed in commission. The quiet which had heretofore reigned in that locality was to be known no more. The emigrant road, or "Oregon Trail" down the Boisé Valley was turned into a main street of the infant city. On each side of the old beaten wagon road the first buildings were erected.

During the summer of 1863, the emigration from the border states to the extreme West, across the plains, was very heavy. The first emigrant train, consisting of forty wagons, drove on to Main Street. The wagons contained families from Missouri and Arkansas, refugees from their home states fleeing from the guerilla warfare occasioned by the Civil War. The teams of these emigrants were halted midway along the street to permit the purchase of supplies. The train then moved on to the bank of the river below the town and went into camp. Other trains of emigrants followed a few days later, and camped also below the town on the bank of the river.

The tent and wagon city they made soon rivaled in size the more substantial city of Boisé. Few, if any, of the arrivals had any fixed destination. Their object originally was only to escape the horrors of civil war, and find a place where they could establish a peaceful home. Arriving at Boisé City, where it was in the heyday of its greatest early prosperity, many of the families wisely concluded to travel no farther.

A number of the heads of the families started out to make a personal examination of the surrounding country, that they might better determine what was best to do. The result was that Boisé Valley was soon dotted with farmhouses, and made cheerful by the laughter of happy children.   Some of the more enterprising men crossed the divide to the Payette Valley and became home-builders there.

Before the arrival of these emigrant trains, Boisé City was almost exclusively a man's town.   The population consisted of at least ten men to one woman, consequently it was not a city of homes.   The young men who constituted the greater part of its population, having no firesides of their own, after the evening meal usually assembled in the saloons, where comfortable seats were provided.   Card tables were always a part of the furniture in these resorts.

The conversation at these evening gatherings was principally about "back home."   While mingling at these socials, I often heard some young man exclaim, "Any man who will remain in this country more than six weeks is a fool.   I am going back to Missouri, and I will be married inside of thirty days."

These young men, of course, were not all from Missouri. Oregon had provided her full quota of the restless element, but most of them held similar views regarding a prolonged residence in Idaho.   It seems incredible, to the present residents of that prosperous state, that there was a period during her territorial days when no persons within her borders planned to remain there permanently.   One thing, however, soon influenced a change in this sentiment.

Among the emigrant families camped below town, it was soon rumored, were several young women of marriageable age.   This rumor caused a noticeable increase in the patronage of the only barber shop in town.   A "shoeshine" stand also was immediately in demand.   The officers at the garrison were petitioned to give a ball in one of the barrack buildings recently finished.   They very kindly consented, and within an hour posters announced that the event would occur a few evenings later.

The plan of inducing the officers to give such a ball was conceived by certain gallant young bachelors whose object was to induce the young men and women of the emigrant colony to appear. The committee on introductions would, it had been arranged, introduce the young Lotharios to the emigrant girls. The plan was a complete success, and before the clock told the hour for retiring many youthful eyes spoke love to eyes that spoke in return. The acquaintances thus formed led to almost nightly visits to the city of tents and wagons below the town. Within one month thereafter several marriages resulted from these speedy courtships. The young men who had heretofore declared that "any man who would remain in Idaho more than six weeks is a fool" were ever after ardent admirers of the country.

The unions so speedily contracted proved, in every instance, to be happily ordered. Pessimists predicted speedy separations, but no such results followed. The young people thus brought to public notice were among the first real home-builders in Boisé Valley, and their children's children are, at present writing, respected citizens of the country which their grandparents took a gallant part in redeeming from the desert — the present State of Idaho.

"The 'shotgun messenger' rode outside in the seat by the driver."

CHAPTER THIRTEEN

BRINGING OUT THE GOLD DUST

THE following spring (1864) witnessed a revolution in not only the means of travel but the class of arrivals in the mining camps of the Boisé country. Roads having been constructed into the mines, stage lines were established. One line of four-horse Concord coaches ran from Umatilla Landing, Columbia River, to Placerville in Boisé Basin; another line of similar coaches connected at Placerville and transferred passengers and treasure to and from Idaho City. The service of these stage lines was daily.

Wells Fargo and Company, upon the advent of stage-coaches into the mining camps, immediately established express offices in all the towns, and provided a means of conveying the gold dust out to where steamers could take it on to the United States Mint at San Francisco. In addition to passengers and treasure, this company carried letters. Stamped government envelopes bearing the company's monogram were used. As government had not, up to the time, provided postal facilities in Idaho, the express company sold these envelopes, which entitled the holder to have a letter conveyed to the nearest post-office on the stage line. Fifty cents was charged for the envelope, which guaranteed the service. This department of the express company's service, though costly, was a great accommodation to the public.

It produced also considerable revenue to the company. Every letter carried out from Idaho by Wells Fargo and Company brought stockholders at least forty cents net profit. Estimating conservatively the number of persons who conducted their correspondence through this channel at fifteen thousand, and supposing that each individual would send and receive an average of four letters each month, the monthly profit would amount to a total of twenty-four thousand dollars. This revenue received for carrying mail was a mere bagatelle, when compared with that received for the transportation of gold dust. But the overhead expenses were at the time enormous.

Every coach carrying a shipment of treasure was provided with a guard. This "shotgun messenger," as he was called, rode outside in the seat by the driver. He was armed with a sawed-off double-barrelled shotgun, carried across his knees ready to repel "road agents." Only first-class men, heedless of danger, were employed by Wells Fargo as guards, and that class of men commanded high salaries. At the express offices where gold dust was received for shipment, the same class of men were employed. All of these were paid high salaries. There were no burglar-proof safes in Idaho during the years 1863 and 1864. Gold dust was kept in canvas sacks in a heavily ironed wooden box. It was shipped in such a box and carried in the front "boot" of the stage under the feet of the shotgun messenger.

Because the charges made by the express company were deemed excessive, many more or less ingenious methods of transportation were devised to avoid the cost. One method, frequently adopted by merchants and other persons who handled large quantities of gold dust, was to send out their "dust" by pack trains. The larger trains were selected for the reason that they were accompanied by a larger force of employees, and consequently more capable of defending their cargo. The packages containing the gold dust were not lashed upon the animals, in open view. They were concealed within the aparajo, or pack saddle, by removing a part of the inside filling. In the space thus created a sack of gold dust was deposited on each side of the aparajo. This generally proved to be a safe method of shipping treasure.

After roads were constructed, freight trains consisting of several wagons, usually hauled by oxen, took the place of pack trains. For the return trip these wagons were sometimes loaded with dry hides at the slaughter houses. Not infrequently an insignificant looking box was loaded in the bottom of the wagon, before loading in the dry hides. Such boxes, supposed to contain nothing but the kitchen outfit of the drivers, often contained heavy shipments of gold. Should robbers have the temerity to attack the train, they could not get the gold without first unloading the hides, which would take more time than prudence would allow. Thus this method also proved an effective means of transporting treasure. There is no record of loss occurring from shipments made by either pack train or ox train during the first three years the Boisé mines were operated, although gold dust to the value of many millions of dollars was forwarded by such methods to the United States Mint at San Francisco.

The discoveries of mineral wealth in Owyhee County

were not confined to placer gold. In the immediate vicinity of the first discoveries, many ledges carrying high
values in gold and silver were located, and within a few
months stamp mills were erected, equipped with the appliances to separate the gold and silver from the baser
metals. While the first quartz mills were under construc-
tion, a toll road was being built, and a stage line was
quickly placed in operation between Boisé City and Ruby.

Gold was also discovered the same year in Boisé River,
near what was named "Rocky Bar." A town of considerable importance rapidly sprang up. Then other
discoveries of the precious metal within the boundaries of
Idaho Territory, on the eastern slope of the Rocky Mountains, caused a rush of miners, business men, and adventurers into that country. From every corner of our country
they came.

Idaho, therefore, before the first year of her territorial
existence had closed, had been widely penetrated. Industry was throbbing within her borders, and a constant
stream of yellow gold began to pour out into the channels
of trade. This gold materially strengthened the credit
of our government, then in the hour of need. Thus the
infant territory, although sending no troops to maintain
the integrity of our nation at this time, did well her part.

A nominating convention in Idaho Territory in 1864.

CHAPTER FOURTEEN

SOME EARLY-DAY POLITICS

DURING the spring and early summer of 1864, arrivals of a different type from those of the preceding year began to flock into the Boisé Basin. These were almost exclusively Irish placer miners from California. They brought no horses or mules with them, but came on foot, having walked the entire distance, carrying their blankets in a roll on their backs, together with a coffee pot and frying pan and a small supply of food. Usually they traveled in groups.

They brought with them a prolonged thirst, and upon arrival in camp quickly made the acquaintance of the social dispensers of liquid refreshment. Having imbibed a few bowls of red liquor, they declared themselves "agin the government."

During the same period the "never-sweat" element in Boisé Basin received large accessions from the northern mines, consisting of "tin-horn gamblers" and road agents. In consequence of the lawless acts of the citizens of Lewis-

ton, who had become so unfriendly as to hang several of
the "boys," and had requested, in no uncertain tones,
that all "sporting men" should leave within a stated
time, there had been a sudden migration southward of
flocks of these renegades.

Many of the arrivals from Lewiston and Florence were
members of the gang of outlaws organized by the notorious
robber, Plummer, and his lieutenants. After the people at
Lewiston had taken things in stern hand, this arch robber
departed for the more congenial citizenship of Montana,
where he succeeded in wresting the political management
of that territory from the Republicans, and electing himself sheriff in the principal mining county in the territory. He then proceeded to organize another band of
outlaws, and appointed his lieutenants as his deputy
sheriffs.

An orgy of rapine and murder followed. Plummer's
lieutenants carried on a similar campaign of lawlessness
among the Idaho camps. With the help of the "agin the
government" type and the indifference of the more substantial element, they succeeded in getting into office men
who, if not actual members of their gang, were at least of
very sympathetic leanings.

In those days — and unfortunately it is the case at the
present time also — our best citizens, who would make
conscientious and unprejudiced jurors, but too often
shirked that duty. When occasion required the speedy
summoning of jurors, hangers-on around the court rooms,
often there for the purpose of being summoned, were called
by the sheriff or his deputies to act as jurymen.

This might even happen in the case of a murder trial,
when such jurors would not subscribe to a verdict of murder, no matter how clear the evidence might be. At the
time the first term of the District Court was held in Boisé

County, there was no assessment roll from which jurors could have been chosen, consequently, as may be understood, the wheels of justice were blocked. No conviction for murder was secured at that term of court, although the local cemetery, across Elk Creek from the city, had already assumed such proportions as to justify the claim of Idaho City that it was a live town.

Election in the fall of 1864 provided for the choosing of county officers, including members of the second session of the territorial legislature, and also of a delegate to Congress. It was noticeable that the sporting class were taking great interest in the delegates who were to attend the nominating conventions that year in Boisé County. It was equally noticeable that the rank and file of our citizens, the business men and those who toiled in the mines, paid no attention to the matter; but few of them even knew when the primaries and nominating conventions were to be held. It was an easy matter, therefore, for the lawless characters to control the nominating conventions of both political parties.

It is doubtful whether any of the population of Idaho, at the time of the election of 1864, other than the Federal appointees, had come to Idaho with the intention of engaging in politics. The saloon interests, to protect their patrons, including gamblers and denizens of the underworld, must see to it that legislators should be chosen who would not enact legislation unfriendly to their business. It was equally important that the sheriff's office should be on "friendly terms with the boys."

Before a candidate for sheriff was nominated, he was required to pledge himself to appoint certain "friendly men" as his deputies. The inhabitants of Boisé County, which then included the Payette Valley, were farmers, most of them the Civil War refugees from Missouri and

Arkansas who had settled in these valleys hoping to be able to make a peaceful living for themselves and families, and had no desire to engage in political controversies.

Then as now there were two political parties, the old Democratic party and the practically new political party called the Republican party, which was then known as being opposed to the further spread of slavery within the United States. The immigrants from Arkansas and Missouri who came to Idaho were, probably without exception, Democrats in their former homes, and while taking no active part in Idaho politics and keeping aloof from the nominating conventions, when election day arrived, like good American citizens as they aspired to be, they went to the polling places and cast what they considered to be a good Democratic ballot. In common with their neighbors in the valley they knew none of the candidates on either ticket. They did not realize that their indifference to politics had enabled political tricksters to control both party nominating conventions, and to place on the ballots as candidates for the respective offices the names of men whom they would not have permitted to enter their homes if their characters were known.

The failure of farming communities to participate in the nominating conventions, however, made no difference in the result. The population of Idaho City alone exceeded that of all other precincts in the county; and Idaho City being controlled by the big business interests, which included the saloons and gambling houses, controlled both political nominating conventions, with the result that all the nominations made were candidates known to be good fellows, "friendly to the boys." Although the gamblers and saloon-keepers took an active interest in both political conventions, yet when election day arrived they were a unit in supporting the most popular ticket. This, owing to the previous influx of Irish placer miners, and the arrival from Missouri and Arkansas of so many staunch Democrats, gave the nominees of the Democratic party an overwhelming majority.

The second session of the Idaho Territory Legislature was duly convened at Lewiston November 14, 1864, for a forty-day session, as limited by the act. of Congress creating the territory. The work of this session was devoted largely to amending and repealing the acts of the first session. One of the acts repealed was "An Act Concerning Jurors," which did not place sufficient power in the sheriff's office to protect "their friends" from the penalties of .the law by selecting jurors friendly to certain interests. A new statute was then enacted under the provisions of which the sheriff and his deputies could secure a jury which would either convict or acquit, as desired.

The records of Boisé County reveal that there was only one conviction for murder during several years following the enactment of this law by the second session of the Idaho legislature, which gave the selection of jurors practically into the control of saloon-keepers, gamblers, and their "good fellows," the deputy sheriffs. It is needless to state that crime went unpunished. Even the one man convicted of murder was permitted to escape.

It is difficult, at the present time, to comprehend how the majority permitted a vicious minority thus to assume control of the agencies of civil government. Numerous as were the criminal class, they were at all times weak in number compared with the sturdy toilers in the mines, who might be depended upon at all times to stand for right and justice, if they were made to see the right side of a question. It can be explained, however, by the fact that the dependable men were not organized. Those who managed to seize control of the government — the gamblers, highwaymen, horse-thieves, and "bogus-dust" operators, with the keepers of their resorts, were the victors because they stood together.

"At this Clark drew his gun and shot the boy."

CHAPTER FIFTEEN

A REIGN OF LAWLESSNESS

To show the way in which justice was administered under the régime of the saloon interests, the following incident is given as an illuminating sample.

One afternoon, two well-known "sporting men" were sitting in front of the "Magnolia," in Placerville, a building dedicated to games of chance and the dispensing of liquid refreshments. A long train of pack mules crossed Wolf Creek into Placerville, and skirting the north side of the Plaza, went out westward on Granite Street. The owner of the train, riding a saddle mule a short distance behind the other animals, upon passing the corner of the "Magnolia," turned into the Plaza. In the center of the square was a well, equipped with a windlass and bucket, approaching which he dismounted, and lowering the bucket drew it full of fresh water. After satisfying his thirst he set the bucket down on the platform outside of the curb, and proceeded to tighten the cinch on his saddle.

While he was thus engaged one of the "sporting men" remarked to the other, "Watch me, and see how I'll fix

120

that fellow." After making the remark, he arose and deliberately walked out to the well, grasped the bucket, which was almost full of water, and heaved its contents over the unsuspecting packer, without warning or uttering a word.

The packer who, like all of his class, was armed with a revolver, instinctively reached for his weapon, although partially blinded by having the water thrown in his eyes. This movement was anticipated by the "sport," who immediately flashed his pistol, and shot the packer before he could draw his weapon. The "sport" proceeded at once to the office of a "regular" justice of the peace, and surrendering, demanded an immediate hearing, which was granted. Before the stark body of his murdered victim was removed from the Plaza, he was acquitted upon the testimony of his fellow "sports" that the packer was first to reach for his weapon.

Boisé City was designated as the county seat of the new County of Ada, created by act of the second session of the Idaho legislature. The city was also made the permanent capital of the territory at the same session. It would naturally be presumed that civil government was well established in that city, as it was the seat of government for the county as well as for the state. The following incidents will give the student of pioneer history a definite idea of the travesty of the administration of justice under the laws enacted by the second session of the Idaho legislature.

News reached Boisé City during the early summer of 1865 that an Indian raid had occurred on the stage line south and west of Snake River. A meeting was called to enlist a company of volunteers to take the trail to recover stolen property and punish the Indians. Subscriptions were also solicited for the purpose of outfitting the volunteers. About a hundred men volunteered. They proceeded to select their leader, and as the result of a ballot Dave Opdyke, ex-sheriff, was chosen. It was found upon canvassing for subscriptions, and estimating the cost of equipment, that only sufficient money was available to equip forty men. Accordingly the man chosen as captain proceeded to select that number from the total who had volunteered. It was remarked that his choice was invariably made of men who were reputed fighters, whose headquarters was in a saloon where games of chance were prominent diversions. However, his choice was gratifying to the general public, as the absence of that number of such men was a relief rather than otherwise. In due time their preparations were complete, and they rode forth, cheered by the onlookers. Though small in numbers, they were an effective-appearing body of men, and we had hope that they would give the raiding Indians the punishment they deserved. Days grew into weeks, while the community awaited news from their brave volunteers, until finally they came straggling in and announced that they had failed to overtake the Indians. We learned a short time later that the company had not even crossed the Snake River. They had gone into camp above the upper ferry on that stream, and having cleared the sagebrush from a quarter mile track, proceeded to test the speed of their horses, and the skill of the men, at that delectable game called "draw." Their provisions eventually running low, they returned as stated to Boisé City and reported their failure.

The following day, after their arrival at Boisé, there occurred a dispute regarding the ownership of a horse claimed by a farmer. At the hearing before a justice of the peace, all the members of the company who were called to testify gave their testimony against the claim of the farmer, except one young man, probably eighteen or nineteen years old, who testified in the farmer's favor. After leaving the court room, the boy was halted on Main Street. After accusing him of testifying falsely, one of the men slapped him in the face. At this the boy, stepping upon the sidewalk, backed against a wall and drew his revolver. One of the men who had given adverse testimony regarding the horse, a "tin-horn gambler" named Johnnie Clark, then took part in the proceedings by calling to the boy, "Shoot, curse you, shoot!"

To this the boy replied, "No. I do not want to shoot any person; I am a boy, and not able to fight men, but I am not going to permit any one to beat me up."

At this Clark drew his gun, a navy revolver, and shot the boy, who immediately fell to the sidewalk, although not incapable of speech. His first words were, "Boys, I did not draw my pistol on Johnnie Clark, did I?" to which some person responded "No." He then said, "I hate to be shot like a dog for telling the truth."

At this point a well-known surgeon, Ephraim Smith, then territorial treasurer, appeared upon the ground. Being told the circumstances, he stepped forward and made an examination of the wound, which was at once determined to be fatal. Turning to the crowd which had gathered, Smith exclaimed, "Gentlemen, this is a dastardly outrage."

Opdyke, who heard the surgeon's remark, took him by the arm and leading him aside, told him that he "had better keep still," saying, "This is only a beginning."

Clark was immediately escorted to the office of the regularly elected justice of the peace, where a preliminary trial took place; the witnesses summoned testified, to a man, that the boy, whose name was Raymond, drew his pistol first, and that Clark shot in self-defense. Public feeling had assumed such proportions during the examination, that a verdict of acquittal would doubtless have resulted in the hanging of Clark, and perhaps others of his type who took an active part in securing his acquittal. The justice therefore withheld his decision until another day, and ordered the constable in the meantime to confine Clark in the guardhouse at the Boisé Barracks. Feeling that public sentiment was getting beyond bounds, and realizing that the city jail was not proof against an assault by the citizens, he took the precaution to place him under military guard.

The excitement of the day apparently passed with the removal of Clark to the shelter of the Barracks. When darkness settled down upon the little city of Boisé, all was quiet, and at the usual hour for retiring but few persons were visible on the streets. As afterwards became known, however, during the afternoon when the Clark hearing was in progress and public attention was drawn to that quarter, a few of the leading citizens assembled at a secret meeting place, and effected an organization looking to the punishment of Clark, and the future safety of life and property in Ada County.

The organization was quietly enlarged during the evening by the addition of the signatures of approximately all the leading business men. As it was unanimously agreed that Clark should suffer the supreme penalty of the law as provided by statute, and as it was apparent that the wheels of justice were being blocked by the lawless element, it was determined to enforce the penalty provided for murder, without unnecessary delay. When it became known that the officers of the law had delivered Clark to the military authorities at Boisé Barracks, to insure his safety against the vengeance of an outraged community, measures were taken to ascertain which of the non-commissioned officers would have command of the guard. He was then interviewed by a special committee, and arrangements were made for him so to arrange his guard as to permit the capture of the murderer without committing violence.

The sergeant, not wishing to have one of his men captured at his post, detailed for that experience a volunteer who, owing to illness at the time his company was passing through Boisé Barracks, had been left in hospital. This young man, who was from Salem, Oregon, was but a boy in years. Having reported for duty, he was placed on post as sentry in front of the guardhouse on the occasion of the predetermined capture. Unconscious of danger, the sentry was pacing back and forth on his lonely beat. Just as he turned at the corner of the guardroom, he was pounced upon, thrown to the ground, deprived of his gun, and after having a gag placed in his mouth was tied hand and foot. The attacking party then entered the guardroom, and without firing a shot lined up the guard against the wall, and securing possession of Clark, hastened from the vicinity.

The captured sentinel eventually succeeded in freeing his bonds and securing his gun. He immediately sent a shot after the fleeing raiders. This aroused other sentinels, who sounded a general alarm. Troops were ordered out, and deployed in skirmish line west of the Barracks, that being the direction in which the prisoner was carried, but his captors had gained such a start that pursuit during the night appeared futile, consequently further effort was postponed until morning. But when morning dawned, the stark body of Johnnie Clark was discovered hanging by the neck from a triangle which had been erected on the ground since occupied by the capital buildings of the territory, and later by the state capitol. This was, as Opdyke had said, "only a beginning" of the stern work to establish law and order.

Ordinarily the summary disposal of a character such as Clark would end the story of his crimes, but an avenging Nemesis appeared to pursue him even beyond the portals of a dishonored grave. Some years after his tragic death and burial, a woman who claimed to be Clark's sister appeared at Boisé City, and claiming the right to remove his remains, had them exhumed and shipped by a freight wagon to Umatilla Landing. The box containing the remains was marked for Portland, Oregon, and after arriving at Umatilla Landing was placed on board a river steamer. Upon its arrival at Portland, no person appeared to claim the box. As was the custom with unclaimed freight, it was placed in a storeroom on the dock.

After an established period, it was offered for sale at public auction to the highest bidder, together with such other unclaimed freight as had accumulated since the last "old-horse sale," that being the name given to such sales. Sometimes it happened that valuable cases or packages were sold in this way, and frequently spirited bidding occurred when likely looking cases were offered. When the case from Idaho was offered, a Jew named Mitchel, who kept a grocery store near the outskirts of the city on First Street, appeared as a bidder, and finally the box was "knocked down" to him.

Summoning an express wagon, he ordered it taken to his store at once. Here, aided by his wife and daughter, he soon lifted the lid. The rushes which had been used as packing being removed, the grinning visage of a skeleton was exposed. Help was speedily summoned and the box with its gruesome contents was quickly removed to the back yard. The police were called and requested to remove the Mitchel purchase; but as no city ordinance existed which required them to do so, they refused to act. The news speedily spread, and the grocery man's patrons and others, impelled by curiosity, began to gather. Passing around the house, as do the friends of a deceased person at an undertaker's, they gazed upon the contents of the rude casket. Among those who paused to look was a man who was present at Boisé when Clark shot the boy Raymond. Being impressed by the likeness of the remains Mitchel had purchased, he wrote at once to friends at Boisé, and learned of the shipment of Clark's body as stated, thus removing any doubt as to the identity of the skeleton.

The police refusing to remove the box, Mitchel appealed to the Mayor and City Council, with the result that he was ordered to bury the remains as quickly as possible, and that too at his own expense. The woman who claimed the body at Boisé had disappeared mysteriously while on the way to Umatilla Landing.

"I selected one of the largest melons I had in my load."

CHAPTER SIXTEEN

THE HIGH COST OF HORSE THIEVERY

The prospecting party which discovered placer gold in Boisé Basin, upon returning from Walla Walla with a larger party to work the placers and establish permanent camps, entered the Basin by way of Horseshoe Bend, on the Payette River. Striking over the divide from the Payette, they followed up a small stream afterwards named Jackass Creek. As this route proved difficult for heavily laden pack animals, an easier way was found a short distance farther up the valley, and a trail was graded over the mountain and a tollgate established. This trail was kept in repair during the entire summer of 1863, and was the main-traveled route connecting the several mining towns with the outside world.

Umatilla Landing on the Columbia River soon became the favorite shipping point for the landing of passengers and supplies on their way to the Boisé mines. During the period when there was no wagon road into the Boisé Basin, pack animals were the only means of transportation, and saddle trains, made up of horses or mules, were

128

the only conveyance for passengers. However, in the autumn of 1863 a wagon road was constructed from Horseshoe Bend on the Payette up Shafer Creek over the summit to Placerville. Another road, which permitted passage of lightly loaded wagons, was opened up from Boisé City to Bannock, or Idaho City, as it was afterwards named.

The first wagons to come over the new road were owned by an Arkansas family recently arrived at Boisé. Reaching Buena Vista Bar, a suburb of Idaho City, they drove on to a vacant lot and camped. Two young men who occupied a log cabin on an adjoining lot gallantly offered to vacate their cabin and permit the new arrivals to move in; they were willing, they said, to move into a tent. As there were two very pretty young girls, aged eighteen and twenty years, in the emigrant family, it is possible that this fact influenced the young men in their gallant action of moving outdoors.

At least some of their cynical neighbors, who witnessed the transfer with jealous eyes, asserted that was the paramount influence.

One Sunday morning a few days after the family had settled in the cabin, I drove into town with several pack animals loaded with watermelons, and stopped to dispose of them on an adjoining block. I was soon surrounded by a number of miners, each clamoring to purchase a melon. The unusual scene attracted the attention of the new family. When the girls realized that melons were being offered for sale, they solicited the young men, who were present, as usual, to purchase a melon.

"Certainly," one of them replied, and running out, exclaimed in a loud voice, "Hey, Scap! Bring us in a melon."

Observing that the party consisted of several persons,

I selected one of the largest melons I had in my load. At the cabin I was confronted by the young ladies already equipped with knives and plates, ready to determine whether the melon was ripe. When the incision was made and the melon proved satisfactory, the young man inquired the price.

"Twenty-five cents a pound," I answered. "The weight is marked upon the rind."

Upon examination it was discovered to weigh thirty-two pounds, — a total of eight dollars. The girls appeared surprised. Back in "Arkansaw," their former home, such a melon would have sold for five cents. They probably imagined that in Idaho it would cost as much as fifteen cents. But the young man was not a newcomer ; he knew that nothing in the camp, even baled hay, sold at that time for less than twenty-five cents per pound, so he cheerfully paid the price and treated the girls.

There were good reasons for the seemingly exorbitant prices charged for garden produce. These supplies had to be carried during those earlier days of the mining boom by pack animals, sometimes over very rugged trails. Even after wagon roads were made, the owners of the first gardens in the Payette Valley did not adopt that method of transporting their vegetables to market. The manifest reason was that while wagon transportation was cheaper, the wagons could not serve in delivering the produce at the cabins of the miners, situated as they were in all sorts of craggy places among the hills.

To reach these best customers of ours necessitated the employment of a train of pack animals. In addition to these pack animals were the work animals necessary for cultivating the soil. Increasing this high cost of production was the loss through thievery of our best saddle animals.

As has been shown, there was during the summer of 1863 no statute in Idaho which forbade horse stealing, or provided a penalty for appropriating the property of another. Our only recourse would have been to follow the trail of the offender. If we overtook our property, a fight was certain to ensue, in which double-barrelled shotguns and Colt revolvers would decide the ownership. During that entire summer the ranchmen quietly and wisely submitted to their losses rather than incur the expense, and probable consequences, of a pursuit which might fail to recover their stolen property or even bring more tragic outcomes. But as there is a limit to human endurance, these harmless and inoffensive ranchmen eventually became a terror to all horse thieves and highwaymen.

The horse thievery which flourished in those days when almost every one had to use horses, was one type of outlawry that struck home with serious force to the farming communities. The losses they sustained, added to the natural hate of the horse thief, which seems instinctive in frontier communities, was enough to make them rise in righteous wrath and clean out this thievery with the murder and other crimes that accompanied it. The long-suffering settlers, however, restrained their indignation until it was made amber clear that they could get no relief from the law-flouting officers, who had got themselves into office through the votes of the denizens of the underworld. One instance of flagrant injustice dispensed by them finally brought about determined action. A brief account of that incident will serve here to illuminate the intolerable situation that obtained in those days. It occurred in 1864.

A certain truck gardener, returning with one of his packers and his pack train from delivering a load of vege-

tables to the hotels and restaurants of a mining town
in the Boisé Basin, made camp one night out in the open.
The next morning he awoke to find that his favorite
saddle horse, which he had picketed near by, had been
stolen.   Search and inquiry disclosed the fact that two
men, who had the previous day been seen casting admiring
looks at the animal while it was standing in the street of the
mining camp, had disappeared.   Further word came that
these missing men had reported that they were going into
Boisé Valley.

The owner of the stolen horse immediately returned to
his ranch, and procuring a fresh horse, headed with one
companion for Boisé City.   Arriving there they made a
search of the feed corrals and the livery stables for the
stolen animal.   It was not found, but they did find another of their animals — a mare, which had been stolen
about two months before.   She was claimed by a restaurant keeper, who said he had been given the animal
by John Kelly, the violinist.   Every one who knew Kelly
knew that he never stole a horse ; he was too fat and lazy
to go out on the range and catch one.

The restaurant keeper refused to surrender the stolen
animal, so the owner was obliged to secure a lawyer to help
him recover his property.   A legal friend kindly volunteered his services gratuitously.   He and a blacksmith
qualified as bondsmen ; but notwithstanding the validity
of the surety, 'which was unquestioned, the justice of the
peace before whom the case was brought, required the
complainant to weigh out gold dust enough to pay the
estimated costs before he would issue the writ.   The
result was that the owner of the animal had to pay seventy
dollars, including a back stable bill, to recover an animal,
which every one, including the justice and the sheriff,
knew was his before any evidence was offered.

"The justice of the peace required the complainant to weigh out gold dust enough to pay the estimated costs."

The owner of the horse entered the court room of that Boisé City justice little more than a boy in years and experience. He came out after having paid unjustly almost the full value of the animal by order of outlawry camouflaged by legal procedure, a grim-visaged man. With no word to any one except to thank the two friends who had gone his bond, he and his helper led their horses down the street to a spot where a group of tin-horn gamblers and horse-thieves had preceded them from the court room, and there he announced that he would like to make a little speech before leaving.

"Fire ahead!" came the response from one of the leaders of the gang.

He did so by saying calmly but with the ring of determination in his words, "I am an American citizen. I recognize no chiefs. I can catch any man who ever marks these regions. Now the next man that steals a horse from me will be 'my Injun'; there will be no lawsuit."

Had the members of the gang who were present been less confident of their power, and given more attention to the glint of the eyes and the set of the jaws of the man who made that speech, they might have taken warning. But in a spirit of bravado, they resolved to teach the "rutabaga peddler" to take a joke.

A few nights later that part of Payette Valley which lies above Jackass Creek, and is now called Jerusalem, was raided. Nine animals were stolen — five horses and four large mules. There were at the time four gardens, or miniature farms, being cultivated in that neighborhood, and the stolen stock belonged to the owners of these gardens. The instance at the Boisé Court, with this added outbreak of lawlessness, roused the fighting instincts of these pastoral people.

A posse of four men was organized, and after ascertaining that the thieves had started to the lower country with their booty, pursuit was begun. Well mounted and well armed, each riding a horse and leading another, these men, fewer in number than the pursued, took the Brown-Lew trail — determined to recover what they had lost, or to lose their lives in the attempt.

They had been gone about three weeks when all returned, bringing with them the lost animals, jaded and worn almost to skin and bones. The story of that pursuit and the recovery of the stolen stock would add many pages to the history of those stirring days; but it will probably never be written; for the men who make the history are seldom historical writers.

It is known, however, that the recovery was made in Oregon, on the Grand Ronde River below the valley of that name. The transfer, it is also known, was not a friendly one; but if any casualties occurred, they were all on one side. Furthermore, on the return trip a stop was made at the roadhouse along their route and open war was declared against horse thieves and stage robbers. Frontier law, in other words, had been invoked to take the place temporarily of the law that had been broken down through the nefarious activities of the lawless.

"In a short time we were able to report the outline of a constitution and by-laws."

CHAPTER SEVENTEEN

ORGANIZING THE VIGILANTES

ON Sunday, the next day after the return of the posse which had run down the band of horse thieves, the neighbors gathered at our house. They stated that during the absence of the pursuing party they had held a meeting and agreed to pay the expenses incurred in recovering the stock. They had agreed further to stand as a unit in the pursuit and recovery of all stock thereafter stolen. It was unanimously resolved that this agreement be published.

Only a few days elapsed after this action was announced when a representative of the settlers in the lower valley appeared. He reported that at a meeting of pioneers held at the "Block House" there, it had been decided to request the pioneers in the valley above Horseshoe Bend to join with them in effecting an organization designed to relieve the entire valley of horse thieves and stage robbers. He further requested that we send a committee, at a time to be designated, to assist in perfecting such an organization. The members of our local organization were called together, and the invitation was accepted.

A committee consisting of two men, myself and a man named Berry, who had accompanied the party which recovered our stolen animals, were appointed to attend the "Block House" meeting to be held a few nights later.

Although young in both years and experience, I realized the responsibility attached to such an organization. Upon entering the hall where the meeting was called, I scanned the faces of the forty men present They were all unknown to me, but their undoubted earnestness and friendly greeting made me feel that I was among friends.

Soon after our arrival the meeting was called to order, and a chairman duly elected. After announcing the purpose of the meeting, he declared his readiness to entertain a motion to appoint a committee to draft a constitution and by-laws for the proposed organization. The motion was passed, and the chair appointed a committee of three persons, naming me as chairman of the committee.

Since that night I have been called to fill many public positions, for which I have often been but poorly prepared, but never before nor since have I been required to perform a task entirely void of precedent. Retiring to the rear of the hall, I called upon my associates for their opinions and assistance; but I speedily learned that they knew no more than I about the form to be used in perfecting the organization we proposed. However, we tackled the work, and in a short time were able to report the outline of a constitution and by-laws for an organization to be known as the "Payette Vigilance Committee."

Since it was recognized that the proposed committee could not hold prisoners for indefinite periods, it was resolved to adopt three methods of punishment. The trial committee was to determine which of these should be enforced. Banishment from the country within twenty-four hours after conviction was the minimum

penalty; horse-whipping was fixed as an intermediate
penalty; capital punishment was decreed for highway
robbery, murder, and horse stealing.

The debates incident to the adoption of the by-laws
brought to my recollection a pleasant evening I had spent
with a very dignified member of the Oregon Bar, who
related to me part of his experience while, in former years,
he practiced law in Arkansas. He told me that if a man
killed another in that state it was customary to summon
a jury; yet it was not really to ascertain whether he had
killed the man, but to learn whether it was a fair fight.
On the other hand, if it was proved that the accused stole
a horse or mule, he was shown no mercy. Among those
present that night at the Block House, several of the men
were originally from Arkansas. At least, when balloting
began on the adoption of the by-laws, it was evident
that they were especially prejudiced against horse thieves,
and those who appropriated their neighbors' mules.

A constitution and by-laws having finally been adopted,
the election of a president and an executive committee speedily followed. The first question then brought
before the Vigilance Committee was that of bogus gold
dust. The member who proposed it urged that as gold
dust was almost exclusively the circulating medium of
exchange, its integrity should be guarded as carefully
as if it were already coined. He declared that the farmers in the valley were being victimized by the circulation
of spurious dust, and that immediate steps should be taken
to suppress the traffic.

Before the organization of the Payette Vigilance Committee, and its arbitrary interference, large quantities of
"bogus dust" had been brought in from San Francisco,
where it was manufactured. The process employed was
to cut bar lead into particles similar to gold dust as re-

covered from the placer mines, by passing the lead through a machine constructed for the purpose, and then galvanizing it with gold. The product was so perfect that it would withstand immersion in nitric acid, if not permitted to remain in the acid long. If not quickly removed, however, the acid would search out imperfections in the coating, and betray the fraud.

A favorite method of disposing of the fraudulent dust was to mix it with real gold dust. It was common practice for persons engaged in business of any kind to use a tin can as a receptacle into which they poured gold dust after weighing it. Such a can was kept convenient behind the counter or desk, and dust thus accumulated was in turn paid out to meet obligations as they arose. At intervals one of the bogus operators would call and state that he wished to leave a stated amount of money, which meant gold dust, for some person whom he named. Deposits then, as now, were seldom refused, and the amount named was weighed out and poured into the common receptacle, where other receipts were added from time to time as collections were made, until eventually the bogus-dust deposit would constitute but a small percentage of the total in the can.

Eventually the person for whom the dust was left appeared. Upon inquiry as to whether there was any money left there for him, the deposit was delivered without question, being weighed out of the common receptacle, the tin can. Of course some of the spurious metal would be returned, but if the person with whom the deposit was made was doing much business, the proportion of good dust in the can would be much greater than the original deposit.

One man, a member of the notorious Picket Corral gang, was named and proved by the testimony of many present, to have passed different amounts of bogus dust at various roadhouses. Accordingly it was suggested that a beginning might as well be made by giving the bogus-dust operator twenty-four hours to leave the country. A motion to that effect was therefore made, and adopted by a unanimous vote. The president of the Vigilance Committee appointed six persons to proceed to Picket Corral the following day and execute the order. It was arranged that they should assemble at Colonel Flournoy's roadhouse at eleven o'clock that forenoon and start from there together. I was named as leader of the enterprise, and given a written order which I was to serve upon the accused.

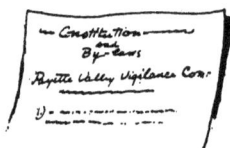

"Seating myself, I engaged in reading an old paper."

CHAPTER EIGHTEEN

ENDING THE BOGUS-GOLD-DUST TRAFFIC

COLONEL Flournoy's roadhouse was situated on the Payette River near where Emmett, Idaho, now stands. It was not more than two miles from Picket Corral. I concluded to proceed to Flournoy's that night, that I might enjoy a good feather bed, and be allowed to lie until late the next morning. After promising the men who were to accompany me the following day that I would meet them at eleven o'clock as agreed, I made the trip, and arousing the Colonel, was admitted and shown a bed.

Next morning upon entering the living room, I found there four members of the Picket Corral gang, one of whom was the bogus-dust operator whom I was to interview later. Passing through the living room without pause, I entered the dining room, where I partook of an excellent breakfast, served by Mrs. Flournoy and her two grown daughters.

Returning to the living room, I found the same company present, awaiting some object. They were all members of an organization of outlaws, which extended from Idaho City to Walla Walla, Washington, with outposts in several localities. I had secured a roster of their membership, taken from a death-bed confession of one of their members, and consequently knew the kind of company into which I had fallen. When I came out from my breakfast the four men were sitting on a long bench against the wall, one end of which was near the outside door.

I secured a chair, which I placed in an opposite corner, and seating myself, engaged in reading an old paper. An hour, perhaps, passed while we held our respective positions, when a new arrival entered the door. A hand immediately reached out and plucked his coat, and a finger pointed at where I sat. The entire Picket Corral auxiliary of the organized band was now present. Assembling in a corner, they consulted in whispers for a few minutes.

Then the latest arrival rose and called me outside. No member of the Flournoy household or other person except ourselves was present, and if a secret conference was desired there was no occasion to seek the open air; but knowing as well as I did their method of removing unfriendly persons, I understood their desire to separate me from the house and any members of the family who might be on the outlook for possible action. The move was agreeable to me. Respecting the family, as I did, I did not wish to have them see men take one another's lives. When I stepped over the threshold of that door, followed by the entire party, I did not expect to enter it again alive; the odds were too great. But I was resolved to leave a record of which my friends might be proud.

No word was spoken while my man and I, trailed by

the others, made our way to a corral near by, constructed
of logs planted upright in a trench. At one corner of
the corral was a set of bàrs used as a gateway. Stepping
inside, I immediately turned my back into a corner against
the posts, and facing my audience, exclaimed, "Well!
show your colors. I am no immigrant; I understand
your object. You are here to murder me, but I do not
believe you can do it. I will make the biggest funeral
ever held in this valley." This declaration was not intended as braggadocio or bluff. Having my back to
the wall, with my enemies closely bunched before me,
I felt that unless they shot my spinal column off, I would
get every man in the party.

"I presume that you know," I went on, "that a Vigilance Committee has been organized, and that their
activities will include the entire valley. If you men
had adopted the tactics of the fox, and left your own
neighborhood to steal horses and mules, it is probable
that the community would never have become aroused.
But no; you became too lazy, and robbed your neighbors,
until it has become necessary to organize against you."

Turning to the bogus operator, who was present, I said,
"By the way, Mr. Conklin, I have been appointed to
serve notice on you to leave the country within twenty-
four hours for passing bogus gold dust."

"Any person who says that I have ever passed more
than $7.50 worth of bogus dust is a liar," shouted the
accused.

"I know persons on whom you have passed more than
that amount, and they were not liars," I replied, "and
you must not call them such."

"Every man has a right to his opinion," he retorted.

"That is true," I returned, "so long as he keeps his
opinion to himself."

Then I produced and offered him the written notice to leave the country, but he refused to take it.

"Very well," I said, "I will read the notice to you, if you have no objection, and I will do so anyway." With that I read the document, while the entire group paid strict attention.

When I concluded, Conklin swore that he would not leave the country, stating that he had friends that would stand by him.

While I was concluding this part of my duty, and giving a hearing to his outbursts, the entire party had passed through the bars. They were standing outside, while I was facing them, when the posse which had been appointed to accompany me to serve the notice on the bogus-dust operator came around a bend of the river a short distance below. Seeing me confronted by men whom they recognized as enemies, they put spurs to their horses and came at a charge. The men had probably but recently served in either the Confederate or, Union armies as cavalrymen, for I never witnessed a prettier movement of that branch of the military service. Approaching at a gallop, they swung into line with their leader next to where I stood.

Saluting him, I said, "Gentlemen, I have already served notice upon the accused. I will get my horse and ride with you."

We then rode back to the Block House. Many of the committee had assembled there to learn the result of our visit at the Picket Corral. It was presumed that the committee to serve notice on the bogus-dust operator would find him at the headquarters of the band, Picket Corral. It had been predicted that the serving of the notice would result in a battle. That service had been peacefully accepted, but it was thought probable that a fight would be made against any effort to compel Conklin to leave the country.   However, at the expiration of the allotted twenty-four hours, when the committee paid another visit to the Corral, it was found that the gold-dust expert had left for parts unknown, as requested.   Thus ended, without expense to the taxpayers of the county, the traffic in spurious dust, and that industry was never revived.

Drafting the challenge.

CHAPTER NINETEEN

THE VIGILANTES ACCEPT A CHALLENGE

THERE was a ferry with a bad reputation maintained on Snake River near the confluence of the Payette. While the owners had never been publicly accused of crime, the crew maintained at the ferry houses bore a very unsavory reputation. However, as there had been no charges preferred against any of their number, it was not contemplated by the Vigilance Committee to interfere with them so long as they conducted the ferry in an orderly and lawful manner.

The crew would not have it this way, however. As if to announce their connection with, and allegiance to the lawless element, they sent a challenge to the Payette Vigilance Committee, stating that there were not enough Vigilantes to take them, and dared them to try it. The receipt of this challenge was a confirmation of the rumors in circulation concerning the characters of the owners of the ferry, and the men they harbored around them.

A meeting of the executive committee was immediately summoned. It was determined to accept the challenge, advance upon the ferry, and demonstrate whether it could be taken. Accordingly a messenger was dispatched for me. The messenger brought a note, stating what was proposed, and fixing Paddock's ranch, the "Big Hay Press," as the rendezvous where we were to meet three days later at two o'clock in the afternoon.

At the time appointed, every member was present. Having been chosen as captain of the expedition, I named Paddock as my lieutenant, and gave the order to march. We arrived in good time at the "Junction House," which was located at the junction of the Olds Ferry and the Washoe Ferry roads. Here I called a halt, and selecting four men from the troop, I ordered Lieutenant Paddock to remain with the other men at the Junction House, until about four o'clock the following morning. He was then to march for the ferry, gauging his arrival to reach it on the Idaho side of the river precisely at sunrise. I would take the four men I had chosen and go on to Central Ferry, where I would cross. Proceeding up the river on the Oregon side I would meet him at the ferry. As no objection was made to the plan outlined, I started with my little squad and arrived after nightfall at the place appointed. Central Ferry, at that time, served not only to transfer passengers and pack animals across Snake River, but for the accommodation of travelers.

After seeing to the care of our horses, my men and I partook of a most excellent supper. The purpose of our visit was not mentioned. After a rest of two hours, at about ten o'clock that night, I called the ferryman out, and asked regarding the possibility of ferrying the party across the river, owing to the presence of large quantities of anchor ice.

"Sure I can take you over," was his reply.

Calling my men, I told them that I had decided to advance upon Washoe Ferry at once. "We do not need the other men," I said; "they would only be in the way, and probably some of them might get hurt."

In accordance with the plan outlined, the horses were saddled, and the party ferried across Snake River without difficulty.

Washoe Ferry was located but a few miles above Central Ferry. Both alike consisted of large flatboats propelled by man power; but while the buildings belonging to the Central Ferry were all on the Idaho side of the river, those of the Washoe Ferry consisted of two dwelling houses, one being in Idaho and the other in Oregon, on opposite banks of Snake River.

The owners of the ferry and their helpers were known to occupy as living quarters the dwelling on the Oregon side. This was a square structure built of logs, with a dirt roof. The walls were without openings, except one door and several small portholes, designed for rifle practice in case of an attack. The occupants of this structure, no doubt, considered it impervious to attack; hence their boldness in issuing a challenge to the Payette Vigilance Committee, and sending copies to their friends, the sheriffs of both Boisé and Nez Perce counties.

A short distance, perhaps two hundred yards, below the ferry there was a bend in the river, where the bank was covered by a rank growth of willows. As the party of Vigilantes approached this bend a halt was called, and the men were requested to state whether any of them were unknown to the ferrymen. One of their number responded that he was unknown to any of them. He was then told that the entire party would ride up to the front of the house, opposite the door, that he should dismount,

" Our men charged into the room and had the inmates covered with shotguns and revolvers before they could make a move for their weapons."

and approaching it should rap and awaken the inmates, who would undoubtedly be asleep at that hour.

"Tell them that our party is on the way to Boisé City," were his instructions, "and that we have come over the Big Slide Trail to Central Ferry, but they could not, or would not, cross us on account of the anchor ice which is running thick in the river. We are anxious to go on at once and are willing to pay double if they will set us across. If they open the door, you are to pretend that you are nearly frozen. As there is a fireplace opposite the door, approach it and stir up the embers, adding any light kindling which may be at hand. The moment it blazes look out, we will charge."

The plan worked as perfectly as if the act had been rehearsed. One of the men arose, and opened the door, which was secured by passing a chain through an auger hole in the door and around the door jamb, then using a padlock to fasten it. The man who had risen, after opening the door and admitting our man, at once proceeded to dress, leaving the door open. The floor was of earth, baked hard, and as our man crossed to the fireplace stamping his feet, the bells on his spurs made merry music. He at once stirred up the embers on the hearth and threw a handful of dry sagebrush on them.

It seemed no longer than a minute after he was admitted at the door before there was a blaze of light in the room. All of our men having dismounted, charged into the room, and had the inmates covered with shotguns and revolvers before they could make a move for their weapons, which were hanging on the wall behind their beds within easy reach. There were six persons in the room, all of whom were lying in bed when we arrived, in the three double beds or bunks built against the wall.

It was not later than midnight when we had control

of the house. As it would be several long hours before
we might expect the arrival of the Lieutenant and the
other members of the committee, it was resolved to divide
our force and the prisoners, leaving part of their number
and part of ours on the Oregon side, and sending the other
part across the river to the house on the Idaho side. This
plan was speedily carried out.

Promptly at the hour set, the Lieutenant with his men
arrived, and with his gun at "present arms" he entered
the house. His surprise at finding the ferry already captured may be imagined. I have often wondered which
were more surprised — the ferrymen at being so easily
captured, or the Lieutenant and his troop at finding the
stronghold already in our possession.

"Greenwood was mounted upon his horse and the party started back down the road."

CHAPTER TWENTY

A TRIAL BY THE VIGILANTES

WE all repaired to the house on the Oregon side. Here our prisoners became hospitable hosts, and prepared a very palatable breakfast of coffee, bacon, and bread. After disposing of it we appointed a judge to preside at the approaching trial. Then we proceeded to impanel a jury from the members of the committee present, swearing them in as is customary in courts of justice. Witnesses were produced, and examined as to the truth or falsity of the rumors which were afloat regarding transgressions committed by the prisoners who were present.

It developed during the hearing that the ferry and its belongings was the property of the Stewart brothers, Aleck and Charley, that they always kept a number of disreputable characters around them, and that although they owned no cattle, they were always well supplied with beef, not only for their own table but to sell to teamsters and others.

It was disclosed also that during the previous summer one of the guests at the ferry was known as "Black Charley," a notorious "two-gun" man, whose only means of obtaining a livelihood was by appropriating the property of others. It was shown that during the time Black Charley was a guest at the ferry, a man who had located a ranch at the confluence of the Payette and Snake rivers had sold his claim, obtaining a good price for it, and proposed moving to California, taking with him several valuable horses, which he owned. Black Charley managed to keep informed as to this man's preparations to start, by sending a boy over to his camp under the pretense of borrowing something.

The next day after the man had started with his horses and the proceeds of the sale of his ranch on the long trail, Black Charley started after him. The result was that the man disappeared, and friends to whom he had promised to write never heard from him again; nor did Black Charley ever appear in Idaho again. There was no tangible evidence offered to show that a murder or robbery had been committed. The evidence, however, was beyond question that the man, having in his possession a considerable sum of money, and several valuable horses, had started across the country for California, and had been followed by Black Charley. That he had failed to write to his friends was accepted as proof of a tragedy. The Stewart brothers, Aleck and Charley, could not have been ignorant of the fact that Black Charley was keeping informed concerning the time his proposed victim was to start, and that they failed to give the man warning was inexcusable, — inconceivable.

Further illustration of the general character of the Stewart brothers was given. It was related that some months prior to their capture and trial, there was a dance given at Miller's Station on Burnt River, and that Charley Stewart, accompanied by a half-breed Cherokee, named Bogs

Greenwood, were present.   After the dance Greenwood and
Stewart remained for breakfast, and being in a hilarious
mood spent some time afterward in dancing a cakewalk,
and singing barroom ballads.   Finally becoming wearied
of entertaining themselves, they mounted their saddle animals and started up Burnt River on their way to Auburn.

The Knuman brothers had begun the building of a toll
road up Burnt River, and had established a camp about
three miles above Miller's.   These brothers had attended
the dance at Miller's, but returned early to their camp.
When Stewart and Bogs Greenwood arrived there, the
Knuman brothers were both in bed, sleeping soundly, and
when called upon to arise failed to obey the summons.
Greenwood then drew his revolver and shot one of the
brothers as he lay in bed, killing him instantly.

They then rode on up the river.   Arriving at the "Express Ranch" they entered the kitchen and ordered Mrs.
Durkee to prepare them a meal.   Upon her refusal, one
of them shot her through an arm.   Her husband was out
on the range and there being no man present to arrest their
progress, they rode on up Prichard Creek to what was
known as "Straw Ranch."

Meantime the news of their murder of John Knuman
had been carried back to Miller's.   A posse was at once
organized, and started in pursuit, overtaking them at
Straw Ranch on Willow Creek.   The pursued at once took
shelter in the willows which grew in profusion along the
banks; but Greenwood was soon captured.   No pronounced effort was made to capture Stewart; he being
but little more, at that time, than twenty years old, was
considered a fool boy who had fallen into bad company.

Greenwood was mounted upon his horse and the party
started back down the road.   Soon after they passed the
New York Ranch they found a juniper tree with a branch

extending out from its trunk. Placing a rope around Greenwood's neck, they led his horse under the limb and threw the other end over it ; then making it fast, they drove his horse out from under him, leaving him suspended by the neck. Charley Stewart returned to the ferry several days later. It is needless to state that he was sober.

The foregoing narrative was related in detail at the Vigilance Committee hearing, by one of the witnesses who claimed to be one of the posse that had captured and executed Bogs Greenwood.

The accused having no evidence to offer in rebuttal, the trial came to a close without argument on either side. At about two o'clock P.M., the matter was submitted to the jury. As there was but one room, it was cleared of spectators, and the jury was left to its solemn deliberations. About a half hour later the door was thrown open and the foreman announced that the jury had arrived at a unanimous verdict. He proceeded to read their findings, which had been reduced to writing, as follows :

"Gentlemen of the Payette Vigilance Committee : We, your jury, authorized and empowered to weigh the testimony offered at the hearing this day concluded, at which Aleck and Charles Stewart, owners of the Washoe Ferry, together with their employees have been charged with certain grave offenses, do find, and pronounce sentence as follows :

"We find that Washoe Ferry, together with all the structures occupied and used in connection with the operation of said Ferry are the property of Charley Stewart and his brother Aleck Stewart, and consequently they are responsible for the manner in which it has been operated, and the acts of themselves and the men in their employ. We have carefully considered the challenge which was issued by them, or under their direction, and published broadcast throughout Idaho, in which they boast that 'there are not enough Vigilantes in the country to capture their Ferry,' and accept said challenge as a declaration of their sympathy and affiliation with the lawless characters whom the Payette Vigilance Committee is organized to suppress. In confirmation of such affiliation, we find that the ferry houses have been maintained as a rendezvous for dissolute and criminal characters, and that in the interest of safety for the lives and property of the traveling public the present management must be abolished.

"The verdict of the jury, therefore, is that the Stewart Brothers, Aleck and Charley, be taken to Bluff Station on the Payette and there held until noon tomorrow, the next day, when they shall be taken to the Junction House, and hanged on a scaffold to be erected during the interim. Of the other prisoners, the man known as Bob Hadley shall be given twenty-four hours to leave the country, never to return. The others, having no connection with the ferry or its management, are acquitted and discharged."

"I called, 'Aleck!' and at that he arose."

CHAPTER TWENTY–ONE

AN ESCAPE AND RECAPTURE

The jury that rendered the verdict in the trial of the Stewart brothers was composed of as fine and conscientious a body of men as could have been called to that duty in any of the older states or communities. Being satisfied that such was the case, I found it difficult to determine by what process of reasoning they brought themselves to impose the extreme penalty upon the Stewarts, while Bob Hadley was required merely to leave the country. (He was subsequently hanged at Albany, Oregon, by order of the court.)

I realized that I was largely, if not entirely responsible for the capture of the men at the ferry, and that if the Stewart brothers were executed I should be, to a great degree, responsible for their lost lives. Consequently I resolved to avoid that responsibility if possible, by permitting the brothers to escape during the approaching night. With that object in view I signalled Aleck Stewart to follow me from the house, down to the bank of the river.

When out of hearing from the others, I stopped and

said : "Aleck, I propose to let you escape tonight, or rather
I propose to try to do so. These men would hang me as
quickly as they would hang you, if they discovered that I
was false to them, or trying to deceive them. I shall do
this, not because I think you are innocent, for I know you
are guilty of wrongdoing, but I do not believe your guilt
justifies the extreme penalty. I realize that I may not
have any other opportunity to converse with you privately,
and I desire to inform you that in case I succeed in liberat-
ing you, that you must not come back at any time in the
future and attempt to get even with any of the members of
the Vigilance Committee; for if you do, I shall go after
you, and help hang you."

While I was speaking, the horses were being saddled
preparatory to starting for our night encampment. Bluff
Station was reached without accident. Here it was
planned that the entire committee, with their two prisoners,
should spend the night at a large roadhouse, owned and
operated in connection with a ferry on the Payette River.
It was a long log building, divided into compartments.
The largest was used for storage purposes, for the owner
was engaged in freighting from Umatilla, Oregon, to the
Boisé mines. Against the walls of this storeroom were
built tiers of double berths, enough to accommodate fifty
men.

There was but one door opening outside from this room,
and besides being locked, it was barricaded by a barrel of
whisky which was placed against it. About nine o'clock
that night I conducted the brothers into this storeroom,
and assigned them a double berth. Having appropriated
a key from one of the other doors, before leaving the room
I unlocked the door, and rolled the whisky barrel back
far enough to permit the opening of the door wide enough
to allow a man to pass out.

It was late when the crowd sought their beds, leaving a young man on guard, but he, no doubt, fell asleep on watch. The other men, having been deprived of sleep the night previous, were soon locked in slumber, from which they did not awake until broad daylight; when, lo and behold, the prisoners had flown. A light snow had fallen the evening before, and the tracks of the escaping men were plainly visible, leading back toward the ferry.

The members of the Vigilance Committee were quickly assembled, and I was called upon to state what I thought should be done. To this I responded that no man, or set of men, could escape if pursued; and that these men had left a trail which could be easily followed, if it was desired to overtake them. It was evident that a large majority of the members were in favor of recapturing the men. Accordingly the horses were fed and saddled while breakfast was being prepared, and within an hour the pursuers were on the trail in pursuit of the fugitives.

It was known to the Stewarts that the ice had gorged in the river a mile above their ferry. They had made for that gorge, aiming to cross Snake River on the ice; but upon their arrival where the gorge had occurred, they found that the ice had disappeared, and continuing down the river to the ferry landing they saw Bob Hadley on the Oregon side of the river preparing his horses to leave the country, his twenty-four hours' margin having almost expired. He was called over, and ferried them across, and they all started for the lower country together, leaving the ferry before their pursuers arrived.

When the start was made from Bluff Station to follow the escaped prisoners, two members of the committee proposed to take the road I had taken with my posse, when advancing upon the ferry. They said that they would go around by Central Ferry and meet the other members of the committee at the Washoe Ferry. I had been observing these men, and was not convinced of their honesty : consequently I declared my intention of taking the same route.

My object was to keep in touch with them and determine whether they were in sympathy with the movement to suppress lawlessness. In the course of a few miles they both declared that their horses were not able to make the trip to Washoe Ferry, and both declared their intention to turn back ; which they accordingly did, while I pushed on. Arriving at the ferry, I found that the main body of men had arrived and were waiting for me.

It was my intention at that time to make a few remarks to the men, stating that since we had accomplished our purpose in breaking up the Washoe Ferry gang, it would be a more pleasant memory in after years to recall the manner in which we had accomplished it if the lives of the Stewart brothers were spared. My plans, however, were disrupted by the fact that L. C. Berry, a stanch friend of mine, had followed the fugitives alone out over the sagebrush plains toward Olds Ferry. Berry had no knowledge of my part in permitting the prisoners to escape, and knew that he could depend upon me to follow and overtake him.

When I discovered that he had taken their trail alone, I called for volunteers to accompany me in pursuit, and at once rode out on the trail. From all the men present, I was followed by three, George Coggin, who owned the Bluff Station Ferry, an ex-soldier named Chapman, and a man named Terry. We overtook Berry some two miles from the river ; he had stopped to wait for me. Our party of five persons then continued the pursuit, following the trail that the fugitives had broken through snow more than twelve inches deep.

At about four o'clock that afternoon we arrived at the

summit from which we could look down upon Olds Ferry, and the foothills on the south side of Snake River. There we discovered the animals which the fugitives had ridden and turned loose to forage on the bunch grass which in many places rose above the snow. A careful scrutiny disclosed a small coil of smoke curling up from a dense thicket of willows growing on the bank of the river. Evidently the fugitives had chosen that sheltered spot to camp and spend the night. They were exhausted, and their horses were fagged out, breaking trail through such deep snow.

A glimpse was sufficient to size up the situation. I proposed to my men that we circle around their horses, keeping out of sight of their camp, and cross the river to Olds Ferry, stopping there all night. The following morning we would hold a council and determine what to do. It was impossible for the men to escape.

We found the river at the ferry landing frozen sufficiently to bear our horses in a group, so we arrived at the hostelry without difficulty. There we were given a cordial welcome, and provided with good beds and an excellent supper. During the night and early morning not a word was spoken regarding our mission.

After breakfast we saddled our mounts and rode out upon the ice, where gaining sufficient distance from the shore to preserve privacy, I called a halt, and addressed my men as follows:

"Boys, it is my opinion that moral courage is as desirable and commendable as physical courage. It is my belief that a party like ours will sometimes go ahead and do what every member feels is of doubtful policy or equity, simply because each hesitates to express himself lest he be suspected of weakening. We are, this morning, confronted by a serious responsibility. I will give you my opinion as to what course we should pursue, after which I shall call upon each of you for an expression of your judgment.

"It is my opinion that if we can recapture the Stewart brothers and Bob Hadley, take their arms away from them and pay for them, then let them go, by this means giving them some money for traveling expenses, it will be better than to attack and kill them. We can kill them, because we outnumber them, and have them corralled. Some of us will probably pass in our checks while overpowering them, but we are certain to win in the end." Then I addressed each man personally for his opinion, requesting them to speak out boldly.

The first man I addressed for his opinion was George Coggin, an Englishman, who was afterwards killed by the Indians on the Blue Mountains in Oregon. He was bitterly opposed to allowing the Stewart brothers to escape; but all of the other men in my party were as strongly in favor of my plan. Coggins was probably prejudiced against the Stewart brothers, because of having had a race horse stolen by a former member of the Washoe Ferry crowd. He had, however, recovered the horse in Nevada, after a long and expensive pursuit.

The decision was to recapture the men, and after paying them for their arms turn them loose again. Then the question confronting us was, how should the capture be made. It was not reasonable to expect them to surrender to our entire party without resistance, for it might look to them as if I had allowed their escape that I might follow them with a chosen few to privately put them out of the way. Since I had proposed releasing the fugitives, and they evidently would not permit us all to enter their camp, I proposed to take the risk and undertake to make the arrest alone. My men would not consent to my entering the willows alone unless they were permitted to approach within pistol shot.

I finally agreed, and advancing until I was opposite their camp fire, as indicated by a spiral of smoke, I called: "Boys!" There being no response, I called, "Aleck!" and at that he arose. I told him that they had best come out and give up their arms, as there was no use to try to get away. He said he was willing to surrender them to me, and did so. The other men then gave themselves up. We estimated the value of their guns and pistols, and found that we had enough money with us to pay for them. The Stewart brothers and Hadley took the money and went their way.

We then returned to our respective homes, carrying with us an account of the result of our pursuit. The news was quickly spread, and proved to be satisfactory to the general public.

" He arrived at our house just as we were about to retire for
the night."

CHAPTER TWENTY–TWO

THE AFTERMATH WITH THE OUTLAW GANG

THOSE of us who understood that the machinery of civil
government, including the minor courts, was controlled
by the lawless element, did not expect that defeat would be
accepted without a struggle, although the Payette Vigilance Committee had succeeded in assuming control of
Payette Valley and ridding that community of its undesir-
able characters. We were looking for an attempt to be
made to counteract the influence of our organization, and
we did not have long to wait. "John Doe" warrants were
procured to include the entire membership of the Payette
Vigilance Committee, and given to the sheriff to serve.
He appointed a large number of deputies to accompany him
while arresting the members in the valley below Picket
Corral.

He made special deputies of the Picket Corral gang, who
were authorized to arrest me, as the supposed moving
spirit of the Vigilance Committee. To accomplish my

164

arrest it would be necessary to make a trip up the river to the settlement above Horseshoe Bend. It was thought probable that I would resist arrest, in which event shotguns were to be the convincing argument. I was known to be at home with my partner, Porter. We occupied a log cabin of two rooms, with two hired men. Our custom, as was common with most of the farmers in the valley, was to retire early. Consequently the deputy sheriffs, approaching after eight o'clock in the evening, expected to find all hands in bed and sound asleep.

The sheriff and his main body of deputies rode out of Boisé City, all armed to the limit. It was rumored that he was to be reinforced upon his arrival at Payette Valley by the Picket Corral crowd. They were to make arrests up the river while the sheriff with the main body of his deputies were to make arrests in the lower valley. The assembling of such a body of armed men as constituted the sheriff's force, in a town like Boisé City, was cause for much speculation. It was boldly asserted by the lawless element around the saloons that it was expected that certain members of the Vigilance Committee would resist arrest, in which event they would be shown no mercy, but would be shot down like the dogs they were.

There was a sutler store at the upper end of Main Street in which the officers from the Barracks were wont to assemble and discuss the questions of the day with prominent citizens of the city, including the territorial officers. Soon after the departure of the sheriff and his company of mounted men, several officers from the Barracks and a number of private citizens were assembled in the back room of the sutler store discussing the probable object of the sheriff's advance upon the Payette Vigilance Committee. It was the universal opinion that the object was to murder some of the leaders of that organization, under the pretence that they had resisted arrest. One of those present remarked that it was a shame to permit the Picket Corral crowd to advance upon my place without warning; that if I knew that they were coming it would be different.

The Quartermaster, Captain Hughes, spoke up: "Gentlemen, I have the best horse in Idaho Territory, and he is in good condition; he is at the service of any person who will undertake to cross the foothill trail to Horseshoe Bend and carry the news to McConnell, that he may expect company. I believe that although there is considerable snow on that trail my horse can make the trip before the deputies who come by the lower road can arrive."

G. W. Hunt, a freighter and subsequently a railroad builder, immediately accepted the Captain's offer. He was soon in the saddle, making the toilsome and dangerous journey. He arrived at our house just as we were about to retire for the night. At once I dispatched messengers with the news to our neighbors, and within an hour there was a general rally at our cabin. After due consideration it was thought to be more patriotic for us to meet the deputies at least halfway, and thus save their horses the additional fatigue of breaking a trail through the snow. Three men were detailed to accompany me. We were instructed to meet the distinguished deputies, and peacefully submit to arrest, provided our surrender would be accepted while we were allowed to retain our arms. In no event, however, were we to give up our weapons before arriving at the court room in Boisé.

It was a little later than ten o'clock in the evening when, well armed and well mounted, we rode down the trail from our cabin. We expected to meet the deputies at any turn of the road, but a hitch had occurred in their original plan. The special deputies had been held in the lower valley until the other arrests were made, causing a delay of twenty-four hours. This gave my party sufficient time to reach the lower valley.

The special deputies were quartered at the stage station from which the Boisé City road branches off from the Placerville road. They were eating their breakfast when we arrived upon the scene. They had stacked their guns by standing them against the house under the porch. As there was no window on the side from which we approached, the first notice they had of our presence was the jingle of our spurs. Immediately they sprang to their feet and made for the door. The first to arrive opened it wide enough to permit an arm to reach for one of the guns, when a hoarse voice sang out, "Drop it!" The order was quickly obeyed. Our appearance evidently disarranged their plans. It was their intention to surprise me the following night at my home, and leave no witnesses.

We rode by the Junction House, down to the Block House. There we learned that the sheriff and a large number of deputies had raided the valley, arresting every person they met, and had taken them all to Boisé City. These same brave deputies, who subsequently murdered every passenger on a stage between Montana and Salt Lake City, failed to attempt our arrest. Their chief, the sheriff, delivered his prisoners to a subordinate court in Boisé City. There from want of evidence they were discharged, and came straggling back to their homes.

The only result was that the taxpayers of the county were required to pay the expenses of the disgraceful fiasco. It was loudly proclaimed by the sheriff and his deputies that they would put the fear of God into the hearts of the Vigilance Committee. Had their plans to dispose summarily of a few of the leading spirits among the Vigilantes been carried out, it would probably have given such local organizations a setback for an indefinite period.

The flurry of excitement caused by the arrest of so many of the best citizens in the valley soon passed over, and a period of tranquillity dawned upon the people, when life and property were as safe as in older communities. But the Honorable E. D. Holbrook, Idaho's delegate to Congress, having failed to read the writing on the wall, and having returned the following summer to spend his vacation in Idaho, met the Stewart brothers in Walla Walla. He prevailed upon Aleck Stewart to come back with him to Boisé, where he would make it hot for the Vigilantes. Accordingly, Aleck came with Holbrook, who placed him under the protection of Sheriff Opdyke. Then he brought suit against me and several others for forty thousand dollars' damages, for running them away from the Washoe Ferry.

Service on me was made late in the afternoon. After I had eaten supper, I mounted a saddle mule, and started for Boisé. I arrived at my destination, Opdyke's saloon and sporting house, just as the porter had begun to clean up the litter from the previous night's orgy. Dismounting and entering the saloon, I asked for Stewart, and was told that he was in the back room, the porter pointing to a door. I opened the door, and stepping inside found a number of men wrapped in blankets lying on the floor. All of them appeared to be asleep except the one at the farthest end of the row. Upon my entrance he rose upon his elbow, and I saw it was Stewart, the man for whom I was looking.

Approaching him, I said, "Aleck, I did think you had some sense, but you have not a particle."

To this he replied: "Well, it looks pretty hard for a man to be run away from his property as we were. That ferry brought us only three cayuse horses."

"That has nothing to do with this question," I answered. "When those men had you in custody, and were going to hang you, I promised to let you go on certain conditions, one of which was that you would never come back and try to play even on any of your captors. I told you that if you did I would go after you and take your scalp, or help hang you sure. Now, from what you have seen of me, do you believe that I am a man who will do what he says?"

"Yes," responded Aleck, "you stuck to me as only one man in a hundred would do."

"Well, then, you withdraw this suit within twenty-four hours, or the chance is that you do not live forty-eight. The hemp is not growing which will hang Ed Holbrook. It is already grown and made into a rope, which will end his activities if he attempts to protect the lawless element from the just indignation of the farmers and miners."

Stewart withdrew his suit, and immediately took his departure from Idaho. My meeting with Aleck once afterwards will be described in a subsequent chapter.

As soon as it became known that Aleck Stewart· had withdrawn his damage suit and left the country, business in the Payette Valley resumed its regular channels. While almost every stagecoach from Burnt River and La Grande brought news of violence and robbery, such events no longer disturbed the peace and tranquillity of Payette Valley. After the first meeting and organization of the Payette Vigilance Committee, a few weeks sufficed to have it become known that a criminal code had been enacted by that organization. From the day and hour that announcement was made, life and property were as safe in the district controlled by that committee as in any of the older communities — yes, safer, for there was not another stage robbery or case of horse stealing in that community until after civil government was resumed by the local authorities. Yet safety to life and property were restored without extreme or drastic measures being applied, except in the case of the bogus-dust operator and the men at the Washoe Ferry, and they were simply required to leave the country.

Dave Opdyke, the first sheriff of Ada County, the officer who deputized the Picket Corral renegades to arrest me for my participation in the Payette Vigilance Committee organization, failed to secure the nomination for re-election. He continued, however, to reside in Boisé, as proprietor of a saloon and feed stable. Besides this, he had business connections with a horse ranch on Syrup Creek, some distance east of Boisé. This ranch, which was remote from any settlement, was used exclusively for pasturing horses and mules, preparatory to driving them to market at Salt Lake City or in California. A peculiarity of the management of the ranch was, that the animals taken for pasture were invariably driven there in the night, and driven off in the night.

The Overland Stage line between Boisé City and Salt Lake City crossed Syrup Creek a short distance below this horse ranch. Opdyke, having occasion to visit the ranch to look after his interests, was caught by several employees of the stage company, including the division superintendent, and hanged. A man named Dixon who was with Opdyke was also hanged. The men who hanged Opdyke and Dixon pinned a placard on their clothing bearing in large letters the three X's which formed the badge, or insignia of the Payette Vigilance Committee; thus giving the general public the impression that the Payette Committee had finally wreaked vengeance on Opdyke. But as Opdyke's connection with the lawless element in both Boisé and Ada counties was so well known, no effort was made by the Vigilantes to correct the impression. Opdyke had a stronger following than any man of his class in Idaho, outside of Boisé Basin. His execution was the signal for an exodus of undesirables from Boisé City, some of whom sought the higher altitudes of Montana, while others joined their friends in Idaho City.

The impression gained general credence that the Payette Vigilance Committee organization included the pioneer farmers in both Payette and Boisé valleys. As it was known that many of those pioneers had formerly served in some one of the armies then in the field, they were pictured as taking delight in seeing a man dangling at the end of a rope. Exaggerated tales were told regarding the prowess of their leaders, including their dexterity in the use of revolvers. Such tales told in the gambling houses in the principal towns in Boisé Basin served as a means of entertainment between drinks.

"They would proceed to sing 'We'll rally 'round the flag, boys.'"

CHAPTER TWENTY-THREE

THE CIVIL WAR OUT WEST

THE Civil War was in progress during the most prosperous mining days in Idaho. As many of the miners had friends, fathers, or brothers in some one of the armies, news from the front was eagerly sought. Owing to the isolation of the Idaho mining camps from telegraphic or other sources of rapid communication, news of events transpiring at Washington, or on the battlefields in the South would not reach the several camps for weeks after each occurrence. Because of the delay, the arrival of newspapers was a matter of intense interest. The *Sacramento Union*, published at Sacramento, California, in those days gave the latest daily reports.

Such news was carried from Sacramento, California, to Portland, Oregon, and from Portland to Umatilla by steamboat and portages, to Umatilla Landing, and from there to Idaho City, and other mining towns, by another stage-coach. At the hour when the stage with the express was due at the several towns, a crowd was invariably assembled at the express office. Everybody was clamorous to obtain a paper; and although they sold for one dollar each, there were never enough to supply the demand. The local newspapers, as rapidly as possible, issued extras to meet the deficiency. The extra containing an abstract of the most startling events was quickly sold out at fifty cents a copy.

Every man who succeeded in obtaining a copy of the *Sacramento Union* was followed as he came from the express office. In a short time the streets in every direction were dotted with groups of anxious men, gathered around the more fortunate possessors of papers, who were obligingly reading the most interesting paragraphs to an eager audience. News of battles won by the Confederate Armies brought shouts of rejoicing from Southern sympathizers. Immediately they repaired to their favorite saloon and began to imbibe some well-known brand of "joy producer." If the dispatches were favorable to the Union Armies, the adherents of Abraham Lincoln and the Union generals quickly evidenced their possession of a consuming thirst equal to their adversaries. In either case the result was financially the same — the saloon keeper was the beneficiary; and not infrequently the undertaker was also given employment.

A stranger coming upon the business streets of Idaho City during those prosperous mining days, between the hours of eight A.M. and eight P.M., would have been impressed by the orderly appearance of the town. But few persons were visible on the streets, and they were generally quiet. Business in the stores and shops was conducted in the same diligent manner as in any well-conducted city. At a later hour, however, the "lid" was off.

Idaho City was "an open town," in all the name im-

plies.   The doors of every palace of vice were thrown open,
and the miners who came to town to spend the evening
amidst more cheerful surroundings than their dingy cabins
were invited to enter.   "'Walk into my parlor,' said the
Spider to the Fly."   There were no other places than those
where liquor was sold, in which men could assemble to
spend a social hour, and learn the latest news from the
armies in the field.   As a result, those resorts were filled
to overflowing every night.

A large percentage of the men who congregated at night
in the various resorts in Idaho City were men who but seldom indulged in strong drink, and another considerable
number never indulged.   But miners, as a rule, are liberal,
big-hearted men, who are willing to pay for what they get,
and being privileged to enter the saloon and enjoy its
music and seats, felt that they should not leave without
spending something.   They would call up one or more of
their friends and invite them to join in taking a drink or a
cigar.

Such a moderate indulgence might not, and probably
would not, under ordinary circumstances, result in a mis-
understanding or quarrel, but as the most prosperous period of the mining industry in Idaho was during the Civil
War, and as both North and South were represented at all
times at every gathering of men in the mining towns, it
naturally followed that the principal topic discussed was
the right of the Southern states to secede.   Sensible men,
if sober, could, even in Idaho, although partisans of different sections of the United States, discuss the merits of
their favorite champions, Jeff Davis or Abe Lincoln, without losing their equilibrium; provided such discussions
took place in the open, when their heads were clear.   But
when the dispute originated in a saloon, where the air was
foul with the fumes of tobacco, and both parties had im-

bibed one or more drinks of liquor, such controversies often resulted fatally to one or both disputants.

General Sherman is credited with having said that "War is hell." Those who have had an opportunity to witness its results are apt to concur in his findings. Certainly Idaho City during the progress of the Civil War was a veritable Hades, and many of the tragedies enacted there during that period were direct results of the partisanship engendered by that unfortunate contest. No morning paper was published in Idaho City, but the waiters in the restaurants who served on the late night shift gave their morning customers, with apparent relish, the events of the preceding night, using but one brief sentence, "a man for breakfast, at White's Exchange," or if more than one, as sometimes occurred, giving the number and place where the occurrence took place.

The first sheriff of Boisé County, after Idaho Territory was organized, was Sumner Pinkham. He was appointed by the Governor to fill the position until his successor was elected. Pinkham was well qualified to fill the position during those strenuous days. He was a man of powerful physique. While yet in the prime of life, his hair was almost white; but his cheeks were as rosy as a boy's. Under other conditions than those which existed during the Civil War, when fathers were arrayed against sons and sons against fathers, he would have been a general favorite in such a cosmopolitan community as that of Boisé County, Idaho. But Sheriff Pinkham was a radical Union man. Having lived in mining camps and other frontier localities for the major years of his life, he had acquired the habits of the men with whom he had associated. While not a drunkard, he was a frequenter of saloons; and while not a gambler, he was not an easy antagonist in a game of poker. He was in fact a typical mountaineer and frontiersman, a capable man among men.   He courted danger rather than avoided it.

It was Pinkham's delight to gather a few of his loyal friends together and enter a saloon where a number of Southern sympathizers were celebrating a victory of the Confederate armies.   Crowding their way up to the bar, he would invite all present to take a drink.   After pouring the liquor into their glasses they would then hold them aloft and proceed, before drinking, to sing, "We'll rally 'round the flag, boys."

The prestige of Pinkham and the friends who invariably accompanied him on such occasions was so generally recognized that the singing of Southern songs and the boasting of Southern sympathizers immediately ceased upon the entrance of Pinkham and his party.   Such episodes frequently recurring, however, intensified the bitterness of partisan feeling, until it was generally understood that there were several men who only awaited their opportunity to murder Pinkham.   The term "murder" is a harsh expression, but no other word will convey the true significance of their intent, as it was well known that no man could be found who would undertake to kill him in fair fight.

It is proverbial in a community of miners, such as Idaho City at that time, that but a very limited number of the population ever take a bath unless compelled to swim a stream.   With the probable object of encouraging cleanliness, Nature had provided a hot spring of generous proportions, about a mile below the city.   This was adjacent to the main-traveled road between Boisé and Idaho cities, and consequently a swimming pond, bathhouse, and barroom were provided.   As the barroom was well stocked with choice liquors and cigars, it became a drawing card, and soon the place developed into a popular resort.   A bus line was established, which made semi-hourly trips between the springs and town. The swimming pond and the bar were the night attractions. A boarding house and sanitarium was eventually established which became the temporary home of wives who had accompanied their husbands to Idaho City. This was located on an eminence above Moore's Creek, and enjoyed a beautiful view of the pine-clad hills to the east.

Sunday was a busy day at the warm springs, although few patrons appeared during the forenoon of that day. Most persons retired late on Saturday night, and as a result they slept late. It became known that ex-sheriff Pinkham had acquired the custom of visiting the warm springs early every Sunday morning to bathe. It was also known that few persons were present at so early an hour. That time and place was chosen by the cutthroat crowd to dispose of the man they had marked for slaughter.

A notorious bravo named Ferd Patterson was selected for the dastardly deed. He had obtained notoriety by killing the captain of the steamer on which he had arrived at Portland from San Francisco. Subsequently he had scalped his mistress. For the latter offense he was arrested by a member of the Portland police, and after a farcical trial, as in the case of his murder of the captain of the steamer, he was acquitted.

He had come to Idaho vowing vengeance against the policeman who had presumed to question his right to scalp a woman. Arriving at Idaho City, Patterson became the champion of the underworld. To maintain his reputation as a "killer," he sought to distinguish himself before the bravos of Idaho City.

He was a man of superb physique, physically more than the equal of the average man, but his forte was to kill, not merely to conquer. He was a gambler by profession, and soon became a well-known figure at the bars and gambling tables. This was precisely the man for whom the enemies of ex-sheriff Pinkham were looking. Physically they were equals; but it was not proposed to have a physical contest between the champions: it was to be a duel to the death, when no witnesses were present except the personal and political friends of Ferd Patterson.

The plot was laid, and on the following Saturday afternoon a man from Boisé, who was another "good fellow," came into Idaho City driving a fine team of horses hitched to a light buggy. Pinkham, as was generally known, was fond of fast driving horses, so the good fellow from Boisé invited him to ride down to the warm springs with him Sunday morning. As Pinkham accepted the invitation thankfully, the hour was fixed, a social glass was taken, and they parted for the night.

At the hour agreed upon next morning they started. As the drive was but about a mile, the distance was soon covered. Arriving opposite the entrance to the bathhouse, Pinkham descended from the buggy, and ascended the steps leading to the veranda, or porch, in front of the building. The man with his team drove on. The entrance to the bathhouse was through the barroom, by a door from the veranda. From the rear of the barroom a door opened into a hall through which access was had to the swimming pond in the rear. On each side of the hall were private bathrooms.

Opening the door, Pinkham stepped from the veranda into the barroom. There he was at once confronted by Patterson, who immediately proceeded to provoke a quarrel. Pinkham recognized at a glance the company into which he had fallen, and realizing their purpose, simply remarked, "That's all right, Patterson," and brushing by Patterson and his party, opened the back door, and stepping out into the hall, entered one of the private bathrooms and closed the door.

The subsequent features of the tragedy I was given by one of the attorneys for the defendant, to whom it was related in confidence. After Pinkham had shut himself in the bathroom, Patterson and his party passed through the hall on out to the swimming pond. Patterson stated that they remained in the pond so long that he thought Pinkham would have returned to town; and he hoped that he was gone, for he knew there was not a drop of cowardly blood in Pinkham's body, and if the ex-sheriff was still present he must precipitate a quarrel with him or else the men who were with him (Patterson) would think he had weakened.

He knew also that if a quarrel was begun he must "get" Pinkham, or Pinkham would get him. For the purpose of getting the "drop" on Pinkham, therefore, while coming through the hall he drew and cocked his revolver, before entering the barroom. Finding that Pinkham was not present, he stepped to the door opening on to the porch. There he saw Pinkham standing at the end next to the steps. He was leaning against a post, with one leg thrown over the guard rail, evidently waiting for an opportunity to ride to town.

As Patterson came through the door, with his revolver cocked in his hand, he made an insulting exclamation. But before Pinkham could turn to face him, Patterson fired. The first shot caused a mortal wound; but Patterson, to make certain of his deadly work, fired the second shot, which took effect as Pinkham was falling.

Patterson immediately mounted a horse which was in readiness, and fled toward Boisé City. The news of Pinkham's murder was quickly conveyed to Idaho City, where one of Pinkham's former deputies, Orlando Robbins, familiarly known as "Rube Robbins," mounted a horse and immediately started in pursuit. As Rube was the lighter rider, or perhaps had the better horse, he overtook and arrested Patterson before he had covered more than half the distance to Boisé City, although Patterson had an advantage of nearly an hour in starting.

Starting back with his prisoner, he met the sheriff, who had also started in pursuit. He brought the intelligence that great excitement prevailed in Idaho City over the killing of Pinkham, and that it was extremely probable that an effort would be made by the miners and business men of the community to take Patterson from his custodians, for the purpose of hanging him. To avoid such a contingency a detour was made, and the prisoner was eventually lodged in the county jail without interference.

"They were men who worked on the night shift at some
gambling house."

CHAPTER TWENTY–FOUR

A RIGHTEOUS DEMAND FOR JUSTICE

THE murder of Pinkham was "the straw which broke
the camel's back." Of the many murders committed in
Idaho City and vicinity during the previous years, the
victims were invariably men unknown to but few personal
friends. Their lives being snuffed out by the bullet of
some bravo caused not even a ripple beyond the immediate vicinity of their mining claims. Inclosed in a pine
box, the remains were quietly deposited in the public cemetery at the upper end of Buena Vista bar, no prayers being
said, no tears being shed.

It sometimes happened that the man who fired the fatal
shot was arrested. In such a case, however, witnesses
were invariably ready to testify that the deceased was the
aggressor. Capital punishment was the penalty provided
by law for murder; but the records of Boisé County,
Idaho, fail to show that such a penalty was ever exacted
during the years of placer-mining activity.

Ferd Patterson, and his friends who were present at the killing of ex-sheriff Pinkham, were all of the class known as "night hawks." They were men who worked on the night shift at some gambling house, and consequently slept during the day. The fact that they were present during the middle of the forenoon at the warm springs was taken by all who knew their characters as evidence that the entire group of gamblers were there for a purpose, as shown by the result.

Pinkham's friends, who were numerous, speedily grasped the full import of the situation. Pinkham had been murdered by contract, the details looking to his murder having been arranged in advance. A few of Pinkham's friends assembled in a private room, and after canvassing the situation, they determined to invite a larger number of men, upon whom implicit confidence could be placed, to meet for the purpose of consultation, in a fireproof storeroom connected with one of the most prominent mercantile houses in the city. The hour of the meeting was fixed for ten o'clock that night.

When the hour arrived, ten men, all of whom were prominent in their respective callings, both professional and mercantile, were grouped in the limited space available among boxes and bales of merchandise. A single candle dimly burning gave light to this meeting. No word was uttered above a whisper, the object being to maintain absolute secrecy. It was well understood that the life of every man present would be endangered if it became known that they had participated in a meeting for the purpose of devising means for the suppression and punishment of crime.

It so happened that I had come to Idaho City that afternoon with several pack animals loaded with vegetables. My presence in the city being known, I was invited to attend the meeting. Admission was gained by passing through a long, poorly lighted salesroom, at the rear of which I was halted by a guard who, when given my name, admitted me to the storeroom. I found that I was tardy, all the others who had been invited having already assembled.

A chairman had been chosen, and the meeting organized before my arrival. Immediately I was presented to those present, but personal introductions were unnecessary, as they were all well known to me — three lawyers, three merchants, one blacksmith, one gunsmith, one doctor, and one miner. I was informed that the object of the meeting was to provide ways and means for the punishment of Ferd Patterson.

It was generally believed that he had murdered Pinkham for a consideration, and promise of immunity from prosecution under the law. All of those present at the time of the murder of Pinkham, except two, had accompanied Patterson to the warm springs, undoubtedly for the purpose of witnessing the tragedy that they might testify at the trial if an arrest followed. Of the two other witnesses, one was provided with a horse and one hundred dollars, and fled the country that he might not be required to testify; the other, being afflicted with a yellow streak, would not dare to testify that he saw or heard any shooting.

Under the existing circumstances no man's life was immune from the bullet of an assassin. It was therefore resolved to organize a Vigilance Committee on the same lines as those of the Payette organization, and I was asked whether we would consider an invitation to unite with a similar body at Idaho City. To this proposal I replied that our members were all farmers, who had certain work to do each day. Living remote from where the action would be required, at or near Idaho City, it would be almost impossible for them to leave their homes and farms for the time necessary to make their assistance valuable. However, if they believed my presence would be beneficial, and I was informed when they were ready for action, I would arrange my affairs to be present and witness the fireworks. With that understanding I left the meeting, and the following morning drove my pack animals out to the ranch to resume my daily employment.

Ten days later a courier, Rube Robbins from Idaho City, appeared at our ranch. Beckoning me aside, he informed me that the Idaho City Vigilance Committee had completed an organization with a membership of nine hundred persons, and that he had been sent to tell me that the Executive Committee had resolved to capture the county jail, in which Ferd Patterson was held. He requested that I be present to give the committee my moral support, together with such advice as I might think proper.

Rube remained with us at the ranch until the following morning, when I accompanied him back to Idaho City. After my arrival, a meeting of the Executive Committee was called, and I was informed that a blacksmith named Gilkie had been chosen captain. Arrangements were completed to storm the county jail, and relieve the sheriff and his deputies of any further responsibility for boarding and guarding the man who murdered Pinkham. Three o'clock the following morning was the time set for the attack on the jail.

The members had been notified to assemble, fully armed, at the outskirts of the cemetery one hour earlier, in order that no delay should occur when the order to advance was given. The members of the Idaho City Vigilance Committee were generally earnest and determined men, yet it seemed clear that their plans were not wisely matured.

However, it was too late to change them. As I had determined from the start of the movement that we of the Payette Valley organization should not become entangled in the affairs of the mining camps, I did not then venture any suggestions; but merely assured the captain that I would be there at the hour set.

After ten P.M., to kill time while waiting for the hour set for the rendezvous, I strolled through all the principal gambling houses and saloons. Business in each was practically suspended; not a solitary gambling table was running; the layouts were covered, and the dealers were absent. In no saloon were there more than two bartenders on duty, and usually only one, generally the proprietor.

This was wordless testimony that the intent of the Vigilance Committee was known to the underworld and probably to every man and woman in Idaho City. The sheriff, as was his duty, had assembled guards to protect the jail. As might have been expected, he summoned those who were in sympathy with the prisoner — the gamblers and saloon men.

I did not start for the rendezvous until after the time set for assembling. On the way I made a detour up the Placerville road, and crossing Elk Creek, came upon the ground from the rear. The night was all that could have been desired. The sky was sprinkled with twinkling stars. The air was fragrant with the aroma of burning pine, as a coal pit was smoldering in the vicinity.

The ground between the sodless mounds in the cemetery and around its borders was occupied by hundreds of reclining men, who were waiting to hear the order to advance. It was a time when human lives were in the balance. The walls of the jail were manned by many desperate men, most of whom were criminals who realized that the success of the Vigilante movement meant not only the punishment of Patterson, but the restraint of lawlessness generally. The profession of the gambler was involved; hence the approaching battle would be to the death. The prison to be taken was located at a corner of Buena Vista bar, about a hundred yards from the cemetery. It was surrounded by a stockade of posts firmly set in the ground. The prison guards enlivened the situation by savage yells and the discharge of their revolvers.

It soon became apparent to me that the captain of the Vigilance Committee had failed to organize his men into companies. They were expected to make the attack in a body; and being undisciplined, this, to me, spelled disaster. I could not permit such a result. A few minutes before the advance was to be made, I mounted a log, and asking for the attention of the men, told them who I was. I said that my desire to punish the murderer of Pinkham was as intense as theirs, but I thought a mistake, or rather a series of mistakes, had been made. First, too many men had been enrolled as members; thus giving an opportunity for spies to be admitted. Second, too many men had been called out to capture the jail, thus advertising the intent, and giving the sheriff a chance to garrison the walls of the jail and prepare his defense.

"You all must realize," I said, "that it is impossible to muster nine hundred men, as has been done, without the movement being known to almost every person in Idaho City. We can take that jail, but it will be at the cost of many lives. I cannot see the necessity of sacrificing perhaps forty or fifty good men's lives for the purpose of hanging one murderer."

At that point in my remarks, some of my hearers exclaimed, "That is the man for our captain!"

The suggestion was immediately taken up by the assembly, and vociferated until it became practically unanimous. The captain then came to where I stood, and exclaimed: "McConnell, I wish you would take charge! This is something I know nothing about."

The moment was pregnant with serious responsibilities, which did not admit of hesitancy. Turning to the men, I announced: "Under the circumstances I assume the responsibility, and issue my first order now, which is for you all to go home. When I want any of you I will let you know. But before we separate, I will give you the following pledge: *Patterson murdered my friend, and the earth is not big enough to hide this murderer.*"

It is doubtful if ever a similar body of men obeyed an order more cheerfully than those men obeyed the order to go home. They quietly vanished from sight. When daylight dawned the cemetery bore no evidence of its recent intruders except sundry flasks, which after serving their purpose had been discarded by their owners. The members of the committee dispersed to their various homes before dawn Saturday morning. Most of them immediately retired for a much-needed sleep.

There were many transient persons in the city who, with hundreds of residents, were early astir, eagerly seeking information as to what had happened and what might be expected. Most extravagant tales were told regarding the members of the Payette Vigilance Committee. Their wonderful horsemanship and skill in the use of firearms, especially of the Colt revolver, was passed from mouth to mouth. During these recitals my name invariably was prominently mentioned. When it became known that I had been chosen as captain to succeed Captain Gilkie, it was generally believed that tangible action was likely to occur in the near future. It was predicted that a party of my Payette friends and I were apt to appear at any moment, mounted on horses, galloping down Main Street swinging our ropes, ready to lasso some horse thief, or other obnoxious person.

Such predictions failed to materialize.   However, it was deemed expedient by a certain element, who had influence in the sheriff's councils, that certain men who were known to be members of the recently organized committee be arrested.   The men selected for the purpose were known to be friends of mine.   It was thought that I would undertake to rescue them.   In such an event a skirmish would ensue, during which I would be a target for an assassin's bullet.   But true to the old saying, "The best laid plans o' mice and men gang aft agley," I did not even nibble at the bait they so generously held out to me.   The men whom they arrested, one being a Methodist minister, had committed no crime.

It so happened that the judge of the district court arrived that morning, and before him they demanded to be taken.   The result was that they were discharged, "for want of evidence."   There was no desire on the part of the prosecution to hold the prisoners.   Their arrest had been for a purpose, known only to those who planned the fiasco. It served, however, to make the situation more tense.   As a spark will often start a conflagration, so it was understood that the act of some drunken rowdy, or tin-horn gambler, might precipitate an upheaval which would result in the hanging of every doubtful character in Idaho City; hence the intensity of public feeling.

"I stepped quickly out in front of him and demanded
that he throw up his hands."

CHAPTER TWENTY-FIVE

SETTLING ACCOUNTS WITH SOME SHERIFFS

DURING the afternoon of the day following the postpone-
ment of the attack on the jail, accompanied by a friend, I
called upon Mr. Gilkie, the original captain of the Vigilance
Committee, at his blacksmith shop on Buena Vista bar.
While in front of his shop conversing with his patrons, who
had brought picks to the shop to be sharpened, and incidentally to learn the news regarding the probable future
action of the Vigilantes, I observed a man approaching
down the middle of the street who evidently desired to
have it known that he was not to be trifled with. He
wore neither coat nor vest, but strapped around him was
a leather belt from which were suspended two ivory-
handled navy revolvers and a large pearl-handled cheese
knife. I asked a man who was near me who the approaching bravo was. "That is Billings; he is a bad man," was
the reply.

Having learned that I was to be the victim of some such

189

gallant, I determined to try his mettle. Waiting until he
was opposite where I was standing, I stepped quickly out
in front of him and demanded that he throw up his
hands. He immediately complied with my request, and
I relieved him of his weapons. After doing so, I looked
him over carefully, and said, "Oh pshaw! You are not a
bad man; you just think you are. I will give you back
your weapons."

This occurred in the presence of a score of men, who
heard my remarks. During the next twenty-four hours,
the news had spread that Billings had been disarmed by
the captain of the Vigilance Committee, who gave his guns
back to him. His prestige as a bravo suddenly collapsed.
A few months later he was convicted, together with three
associates, of robbing a stage carrying United States mail,
and sentenced to a long term at San Quentin. One of
Billings' associates in this robbery, which was but one of
a series of like affairs in which they participated, was John
Wheeler, who was an apparently active member of the
Idaho City Vigilance Committee. Doubtless he had be-
trayed their intended movements.

On the following Saturday night most of the gambling
tables were ready for business; but few of their former
patrons appeared, and nearly all the saloons closed early.
By Sunday morning the streets presented the same quiet
Sabbath-day appearance observable in well-regulated
Eastern cities. Conditions were tranquil on the surface,
but an eruption was pending.

During the forenoon of this day, a friend of mine requested me to ride with him a few miles to where he owned
and was working a placer claim. After looking over the
claim, we were invited by the men in charge to remain for
dinner, an invitation which we cheerfully accepted. After
we had finished our dinner, we started back for Idaho City.

When we had proceeded about half the distance, we met a courier, J. C. Henly, a lawyer, on a foaming steed, who urged me to return as quickly as possible. A large number of miners, he said, had assembled at Gilkie's blacksmith shop, and were discussing matters relative to the failure of the civil authorities to punish criminals. Sud-‧ denly the sheriff appeared and told them that he would give them thirty minutes in which to disperse, or he would arrest them all.

I spurred up my horse, and arrived upon the ground before the expiration of the time. I found that instead of complying with the sheriff's order to disperse, the men were throwing up breastworks with the intention of defending their position. The sheriff, in full view, was placing his men in position to descend upon the stubborn miners who, as he well knew, had committed no crime. As American citizens they had a right peacefully to assemble, but he had been urged on to precipitate a collision between his deputies and the miners, and realized that only extreme measures would quell the clamor for the punishment of criminals. If a few men could be killed in an attempt to resist arrest, it might strike terror to the hearts of others; especially if some of the leaders in the Vigilante movement were victims.

Upon my arrival, I took in the situation at a glance. The position of the barricade, I saw, was not well chosen. I knew that on the opposite side of Moore's Creek, on a peninsular point, there was a large ditch, into which water had not been turned. Turning to the men, I exclaimed: "Boys, this is not a good place to defend. I know a better one. All who are armed, follow me!"

Immediately I started for the point I had selected, the ditch which I knew would prove to be a splendid breastwork. From this it would be difficult, if not impossible, to dislodge my men. As my followers crossed the narrow footbridge spanning Moore's Creek I counted them, and found that there were forty-five in all. Halting them in front of the embankment bordering the ditch, I threw them in line, and divided them into three squads. Rube Robbins was placed in charge of one squad, Al Hawk in charge of another, while I took the third. I selected the center. Rube, with his men, was to protect my right, while Hawk guarded the left flank.

I had barely time to make these dispositions before the sheriff and his men came on to Moore's Flat, within hailing distance from where I stood. I ordered them to halt; and if they had a leader, for him to come forward and talk business. If not, they must not approach any closer.

A horseman passed through their lines, and approaching me declared : "The only terms I have to propose to ye, is that you stack your arms and disperse, or the last divil of you will be kilt."

To this typical proposal, I responded, "The deuce you say ; what is your name ? "

He said his name was Gorman, and that he was under-sheriff. I told him to return to his men as speedily as possible, and send his chief up to do the talking, that he could not settle anything.

The sheriff, who was James I. Crutcher, came as I requested, and his first exclamation was, "McConnell, cannot this thing be stopped ? "

To his query I responded that it was already stopped, and added the question, "Do you not think we have chosen a very good place ? " Continuing, I said : "Mr. Crutcher, I respect your duty as an officer, and if you had a warrant calling for my arrest or the arrest of any of these men, and had come yourself, accompanied by a posse of respectable citizens, I, or any of those with me would submit without demur; but instead of such men as would add dignity to the sheriff's office you have as deputies all the cutthroats in the country."

To this the sheriff responded, "When I choose men whom I expect to have fight, I choose fighting men."

"I am glad to hear you make that statement," I returned; "there always had been a doubt in my mind, as to whether horse thieves, highwaymen, and murderers could fight better than good citizens; now we have an opportunity to test the matter. You have about seventy men, and I have approximately the same number. The responsibility rests upon you; it is up to you to fire the first shot. But for your information I will state that if that shot is fired, neither you nor any of your men will cross that flat alive."

He then informed me that I looked upon the matter in a wrong light, and that if we would surrender our arms, we might all go home.

In reply to this proposal, I replied : " You probably have observed that I am armed with a beautiful rifle, a gold-mounted Henry. This gun was sent to me by a friend in Centerville, when he learned that I was chosen captain of the Vigilantes. He thought when he sent the gun to me, that I would not give it up while I lived; and I cannot. Neither will I ask my men to surrender their weapons to such a band of assassins, as you practically admit your deputies are. You have sent E. D. Holbrook, delegate to Congress from Idaho, with a posse, around the point with the object of gaining my rear. I have some boys over there who will hurt him, and we will have to elect another delegate. You had best call Holbrook and his men back, and return to town with your entire force, before further trouble is precipitated." I assured him that it was not my intention to attack the jail. "We have concluded to let Patterson go to trial," I said, "and be acquitted, as was arranged prior to the murder, but his punishment will follow later."

After the foregoing assurance, the sheriff ordered his men to return to the jail, and immediately discharged all of them except his regular prison guards. The men who were with me also dispersed to their several employments. By the next morning, Monday, excitement had subsided, and business was resumed.

A few weeks later Ferd Patterson was arraigned for the murder of Pinkham. As was expected, he was not convicted. It was generally understood that the verdict was determined before the crime was committed, so but few persons were present in the court room to witness the proceedings. A promise had been made that Patterson would receive punishment, and he did, but not just as had been expected.

Soon after his acquittal, the freed murderer left Idaho City, under the escort of friends, who accompanied him to Boisé City. There he took passage on a stage for Walla Walla, where his Nemesis overtook him. The policeman who arrested him at Portland, Oregon, for scalping his mistress, and upon whom Patterson had sworn vengeance, was at Walla Walla when the stage arrived on which Patterson was a passenger. Seeing him alight, proceed up the street, and enter a barber shop, the former officer followed him in, and finding him seated on a chair, shot him. The victim was given no chance. However, as Patterson had set the example of that style of vengeance, but little sympathy was expressed for him and that only by his class.

The intervention of the Portland policeman relieved the Idaho City Vigilantes of a disagreeable obligation, but Patterson's friends in Idaho City generally believed that the Vigilance Committee was responsible for the shot which killed their champion. It was universally known what the captain of that organization had said to the sheriff. No effort was made to undeceive the friends of Patterson regarding the responsibility for his death. The result was a general exodus of the outlaw element.

Many of these, before coming to Boisé County, had been associates of the notorious bandit Plummer, while he terrorized the mining camps in northern Idaho. News arrived that Plummer, having organized a band of choice spirits in Montana, had succeeded in getting himself elected sheriff in one of the most populous and wealthy counties in that territory. His former associates and pupils in Lewiston, Orofino, and Florence, discouraged by the unfriendly acts of the Idaho Vigilantes, resolved to join Plummer in Montana, and share his prosperity and popularity in that promising field.

But alas! The spirit of unfriendliness which had caused Plummer and his satellites to migrate into Montana had also permeated that commonwealth. A Vigilance Committee more sanguinary in its methods than those in Idaho was soon organized there. Plummer, the outlaw sheriff, was caught and hanged, and his Idaho City contingent, to the last man of them, were likewise given the "hangman's noose." The way of the transgressor became hazardous in the Territory of Montana.

"Two members of the committee were provided with ample
money, and dispatched in pursuit of the bandits."

CHAPTER TWENTY–SIX

HOW "ROBBERS' ROOST" GOT ITS NAME

An instance will show the desperate nature of the characters with whom the Vigilantes had to deal. It will
serve also to show the desperate determination to rid the
West of these murderous outlaws.

Certain Montana merchants, having accumulated a
large quantity of gold dust, determined that they would
not pay Wells Fargo and Company the express charges
demanded. Believing that the danger from road agents
had been reduced to a minimum, by the hanging of all
persons known to follow that vocation, they chartered
a six-passenger coach from the stage company. It was
agreed that no passengers should be taken on that special
coach, other than themselves.

The stage company, to comply with this contract to
run a special coach, was obliged to provide for a change
of horses at certain stations along the line. An extra
driver was also engaged to pilot the special over the road.
In making the necessary preparations along the line for

this special coach, all the employees became aware of its purpose. They also knew that the expected party of merchants would bring with them a large quantity of treasure. The driver assigned to take charge of the special had been in the employ of the stage company as a driver for several months, and had the reputation of being one of their most prudent and trustworthy men. He was informed that if an extra coach was sent over the road, he would be given the post of driver.

The denizens of Picket Corral, in Payette Valley, after their failure as deputy sheriffs, had mysteriously disappeared. Now, again, they appeared prominently in the limelight. At the time negotiations were pending between the Montana merchants and the stage company, they were in camp in a secluded nook on the Port Neuf River, the place which later became known as "Robbers' Roost."

As later developments proved, these desperados were in communication with the man who was to drive the coach containing the Montana merchants and their treasure. The Salt Lake City and Montana stage passed by the place where these former deputy sheriffs were in camp. It was arranged with the driver that he should wear a red handkerchief around his neck on the day when the expected party was on the stage; the robbers would do the rest.

Accordingly they selected a favorable location for their purpose, and concealing themselves, waited for the fateful signal. When it came they rose from their recumbent position, and without demand or warning, discharged shotguns loaded with buckshot into the coach, killing every man on board, except their accomplice, the driver, and a little bartender named Jimmie Brown, whom the driver had permitted to ride between stations.

Jimmie escaped only because the robbers had discharged both barrels of their guns into the body of the coach. At this he jumped from his seat by the driver to the ground, and gained the shelter of the brush. As he ran for shelter, they fired at him with their revolvers, but failed to hit him. Eventually he arrived at one of the stage stations, and gave the first account of the tragedy. It was considered reliable, although he could give no description of the men who fired into the stage. He probably owed his escape to the fact that the four horses, frightened by the shooting, stampeded down the road some distance before the driver could bring them under control. The bandits pursued the stage, with the treasure, rather than the fugitive, Jimmie Brown; otherwise he too would have perished.

The daily stage for Helena met the special, with its gruesome load of passengers, a few miles beyond the scene of the massacre, but the treasure was not there; it had all disappeared, along with the robbers. The lifeless bodies of the murdered men were transferred to the regular stage, and returned to their former homes. The special, saturated with their blood, was driven on by the same driver to Salt Lake City. There he, claiming nerve shock, asked for a lay-off for a few weeks, which the stage company granted.

When the bodies of the unfortunate men arrived at their destination, and the story of their foul murder was made known, intense excitement and indignation prevailed. A meeting of the executive committee of the Vigilance Committee was immediately called. It was resolved that the dastards who were guilty of the cowardly crime should be pursued, captured, and punished as the act merited, regardless of time required or expense involved. Two members of the committee, who had formerly served as

"They rose, and without demand or warning, discharged shotguns loaded with buckshot into the coach."

special detectives for the organization, were provided with ample money, and dispatched in pursuit of the bandits.

The detectives went first to Salt Lake City. Without making their mission or presence known, they located the driver. One of them managed to ascertain the class of men with whom he associated, and about the amount of money he was spending. At the expiration of three weeks the former driver asked to be reinstated. The stage company took him back, and put him at work driving, as before the tragedy; he had apparently recovered from the shock. After driving a few weeks, he quit again, and went to Denver, Colorado, where he indulged in a protracted debauch, during which he spent more money than a stage driver is supposed to possess. He was shadowed during this period of his enjoyment by the detectives, each taking turns in his pursuit.

Their quarry had established friendly relations with a woman who lived at the outskirts of the city. One night as he was heading in her direction, both of the detectives kept him in sight. As he gained a remote section of the city where buildings were far apart, they rushed upon him, and throwing a sack over his head, they tied his arms; then they led him to a convenient grove of trees. There in the shadow they proceeded to question their captive concerning the men who robbed the stage. As expected, he professed profound ignorance of their identity; but his lavish expenditure of money during his stay in Denver was sufficient to convince his captors that he was lying.

They threw a noose around his neck, and throwing the other end of the rope over a limb, drew their captive up until he dangled from the limb. They allowed him to remain suspended but an instant, and let him down.

When he realized that lying would not save him, he threw himself upon their mercy, and told the story. He even confessed to the share he received for the part he had taken, and named every one of the murder party. He had become acquainted with them, he said, when they occupied the Picket Corral in Payette Valley.

Having accomplished their purpose, the detectives concluded the exercises of the evening by returning their captive to the branch from which they had lowered him. The victim of an avenging Nemesis was left hanging among the whispering leaves of the branches. Thus the first one of the band paid the extreme penalty for his crime.

The detectives, with the names of the principals in the shocking tragedy in hand, now directed their efforts to their capture and punishment. Taking the Overland Stage, they returned to Salt Lake City, and from there took passage on the Montana stage to the scene of the murder. Although several weeks had elapsed since the deed had been perpetrated, it was not difficult to discover the direction taken by the fleeing murderers, as no rain had fallen to obliterate their tracks.

With two saddle horses and a pack animal, together with camp equipage, including provisions enough to last two men several weeks, the detectives took up the trail of their intended victims. Evidently the murderers had headed for Nevada, and having a start of so many weeks before pursuit was begun, were able to enter Virginia City, Nevada. There, it was found, after disposing of their outfit and purchasing each a new suit of clothes, they had departed on separate trails.

Pursuit was now limited to the trailing down of one man at a time. Fortunately for the pursuers, their quarry did not seek the shelter of populous cities. Each, disguised as a prospector, took his way to different mining camps throughout the interior of the state. The detectives, with dogged determination, kept up their relentless search throughout the state of Nevada and the territories of Utah, Arizona, and New Mexico. Finally the long hunt was ended in northern California, with the capture of the only remaining member of the murderous quartette.

Recorded in the secret archives of the Montana organization is the tragic story. The persistence of those human bloodhounds, written in detail, would seem incredible. Often hungry, and at other times almost perishing from thirst, they braved the dangers of desert, mountain, and flood for more than two years before their avenging task was done. The most confidential relations existed between the Montana and the Payette orders of Vigilantes, and as a member of the Payette organization I was given from time to time the reports of the pursuit of the former residents of Picket Corral.

Today the hurrying trains passing over the Oregon Short Line Railroad bear scores of curious passengers. Gazing out of the car windows on the lava rocks in Port Neuf Cañon, they sometimes question the porter as to why the name "Robbers' Roost" clings to the place. But few of those functionaries, if any, can give the desired information, and it is doubtful whether the present officers of the railroad company have knowledge of the origin of the name.

Writing this synopsis of events of more than half a century ago, I can hardly realize that human beings could have been so inhuman. The civil authorities, at that time, no matter how earnest their endeavor, could not have pursued and captured the Port Neuf robbers. It was fortunate that other means were available.

The relentless pursuit and final capture of those fiends was a salutary warning to others. The genus "bravo" ceased to terrorize his fellow men in that region. When the curtain was rung down upon a period of lawlessness by the extermination of the last remaining member of the gang who perpetrated the Port Neuf murder, civil government was restored. Within a short space of time, both Montana and Idaho were being peopled by a sturdy, home-building pioneer stock, — the men and women who were to remain permanently in the West.

"The men gathered around me and, with hearty handshakes, uttered the Western word of farewell."

CHAPTER TWENTY-SEVEN

CALLED INTO CIVIL SERVICE

DURING that fall, while digging potatoes, I received a letter from the district judge, Milton Kelly, at Boisé City. In it he informed me that the United States Marshal, Major Alvord, had recently visited Boisé. While there he had rented and furnished a suite of rooms for office quarters; and had appointed me his deputy in that district. The judge explained that Major Alvord was engaged in the mercantile business at Florence. Some of his Eastern friends had secured his appointment as marshal without his knowledge, and it would be impossible for him to close his business before the end of about a year from the date of my appointment as his deputy. During the interim, therefore, the deputy must assume the entire responsibility of conducting that office, practically independent of his chief. The judge urged that I take the position, and come to Boisé City as soon as I could arrange my affairs.

Porter and I had enlarged our farming operations during the second year, until it became necessary for us to employ several men and a male cook. Our ranch was a typical aggregation of bachelors — all good men, but sorely in need of the refining influence of a wife or mother. To say that I was tired of our method of living — tired of our food, tired of the vulgarity of our surroundings — would but feebly express my desire for a change.

Upon receipt of the letter announcing my appointment at Boisé City, I began negotiations for the sale of my interest in the ranch. A purchaser was soon found. I wound up my business affairs at the ranch, and settled down to spend my last night with Porter and the men. It was then that I began to realize that the old log shack held many memories for me. Although often discontented, and dissatisfied with my lot, yet I had become attached to the place and all its belongings. The horses, the mules — to all of which we had given names — each held a place in my affections.

The dog, "Tiger," had come to us in the days of his puppyhood, the first year, while Porter and I were still living in a tent. Tiger was permitted to sleep inside, at our feet. By the time winter approached, he had grown to be a large dog. No doubt he felt it his duty, as a big doggie, to protect his two bachelor masters.

The locality was infested with coyotes, which came prowling around our tent at night, looking for something to eat. Tiger would charge out of his bed and pursue the marauders. But alas for the courage and chivalry of poor Tige! when the coyotes had led him away from our protection, they would turn upon him, and he became the pursued instead of the pursuer. With the coyotes a close second, he would come pell-mell back to our tent. Into it he would dart; and, not satisfied with the safety of his bed at our feet, would run over our bodies in his fright, and endeavor to gain shelter under our blankets. Porter always kept a Harper's Ferry Yager close to his hand. One shot from that would disperse the hungry brutes, and make Tige love his masters still more, if possible.

The last night I spent with Porter and the men who had often proved their loyalty to our interests was so replete with memories of the preceding years, that for many hours I courted sleep in vain. I was awake, however, with the dawn. As there was no baby to awaken, or invalids to disturb, the men, while engaged in making their morning toilet, gave vent to their vitality by indulging in songs. The style and harmony of these would not have been acceptable in a fashionable drawing room; but they were a happy lot of young men, whose lives had been spent in the open.

We were soon called to breakfast, after which, my horse having been saddled and brought to the door, the men gathered around me and, with hearty handshakes, uttered the Western word of farewell, "So long." Tige too, now grown to be quite an old and sedate dog, realizing that something unusual was taking place, crowded his way to my side. Pushing his cold nose into my hand, with speaking eyes he gave mute expression to his regret that I was quitting the ranch.

When good-bys had been said, I started for Boisé, arriving there in time for a home dinner, cooked by Mrs. Smith, and served by her daughter. Judge Kelly came for me soon after dinner, and escorted me to the marshal's office. My new quarters consisted of two rooms; the front room was furnished as an office, the back room as a bedroom. The building was a wooden structure, two stories in height. Entrance to the upper story was gained from an outside stairway. The marshal's office occupied one-half of the

" I proceeded to make myself at home in my new quarters."

lower story front, the other half being devoted to an office for the clerk of the Supreme Court. The upper story was used as a Masonic lodge room.

I made it my first duty to become acquainted with the officers, including those of the territory, the county, and the United States. The district judge kindly accompanied me to the respective offices and made the introductions. After meeting and being presented to the officers, I called upon the editor of the *Boisé Statesman*, a semi-weekly paper then published in the city. The editor, James Reynolds, together with his entire force, proved a very friendly and entertaining company of gentlemen.

Next I sought the offices of the practicing attorneys. Some of them were glad to make my acquaintance, and welcomed me to the city. Others, of whom there were several, treated my advances of friendship rather coolly. Upon my inquiring as to the cause of their evident hostility, the judge informed me that they were verbal supporters of the Southern Confederacy. Instinctively they were unfriendly to all United States officers, although, with the exception of one, or perhaps two, I would find them to be honorable gentlemen. The prediction made by the judge proved to be true. The representatives of the Ada County bar, with the exceptions he named, were a credit to the profession of law.

I then proceeded to make myself at home in my new quarters and to wait for something to turn up. I did not have to wait long, however. Soon after my arrival at Boisé City, the regular fall term of court convened at the county seat of Owyhee County. At that term Judge Kelly was required to try a rather heated mining case. His decision seemed fair enough to disinterested persons, but certain men who were stopped from getting ore denounced the judge for his decision. Threats were even made against his life.

As well-known gunmen were being imported by the contestants, I was ordered to proceed to Owyhee County, and escort his honor from Ruby to his home at Boisé City. Under the guise of bringing an escaped prisoner back to Boisé I made the trip. The judge was disposed to conceal the fact that his life was endangered in consequence of his doing his duty. The return trip was made in safety, and I delivered my prisoner to the authorities from whom he had escaped.

Incidents connected with that, my first entrance into Owyhee County, and return therefrom, remain vivid in my memory. Ruby City, the county seat of Owyhee County, was about sixty miles distant from Boisé. A daily stage carried mail and passengers. The "stage" consisted of a small Concord coach drawn by four under-sized and apparently underfed cayuse horses. They were driven by a typical Jehu, named Barnes. The hour of departure from Boisé was three A.M.

Although rated as a seven-passenger coach, the stage was loaded on the morning of my journey with eleven passengers, three on each seat inside and two outside with the driver. I was unfortunate enough to obtain one of the front seats, so I had to ride backward. This would not have been so disagreeable if I could have sat upright; but to economize space, the seat for the driver and outside passengers extended back over the front seat several inches, requiring those who occupied that seat to lean forward.

The passengers that morning were four hurdy-gurdy girls and their chaperon, going to fill an engagement at Silver City, a postal inspector from Salem, Oregon, several others of unknown callings, and myself. I doubt whether a more cosmopolitan group of persons were at any time crowded into so small a space, and compelled to remain in such a cramped position for sixteen hours.

The chaperon proved to be a veritable dragon. When addressed by one of the passengers, she only stared in reply. When speaking to her girls, she always addressed them in German. She early commanded them to refrain from speaking to any of us. They were quite pretty girls. If they had been permitted to converse with the other passengers, most of whom, like myself, were bachelors, we would not have felt the crowded condition of the stage so keenly.

Soon after daylight had dawned, a change of horses was made at Stone Corral. In the station house, a low structure of rough lava rock, we were given breakfast. The dining room, which served also as the kitchen, contained a table so small that we had to sit more closely, if possible, than in the stage. Our breakfast consisted of fried bacon, cooked rare, sour-dough bread, stewed dried apples, and coffee without cream or sugar. The price was $1.50 each. But we were all hungry enough to relish it and forget the price.

I stood by, observing the landlord while he collected the price of the breakfast from each of my fellow passengers.

"Our host by this fraudulent method collected two
dollars for each breakfast."

The chaperon, and some of the others paid in coin; but
the rest paid in gold dust. It was the latter payments
that interested me. Having been accustomed to weighing dust in small quantities, I had become very expert in
judging the weight of small amounts of the precious metal.
In addition to being expert in that line, I was aware that
it was common practice for a certain class of "dive keepers" to fix the gold-dust scales by having a small plate
of copper brazed on the under side of the weight pan,
thus requiring more dust to balance it. Our host at Stone
Corral station by this fraudulent method collected two
dollars for each breakfast when his price was only one
dollar and a half.

After witnessing the operation, I paid for my breakfast
in coin. Calling our host aside, I placed my hand affec-
tionately upon his shoulder, and said, "Don't do it again."

Assuming an air of surprise, he asked what I meant.

"You know what I mean," I replied quietly. "I do not
intend to arrest you for this morning's transaction, but
I shall return in a few days, and if I find you still practicing the same species of graft, I will take you in."

If I had been on my way to Boisé, instead of to Owyhee
County, I would have taken him then, and his gold scales

with me, but I could not turn back with him. When I came back, I found a new set of scales installed.

A fresh team was hitched to the coach, we resumed our seats, and with a grand flourish of speed, were off for Ruby. The day passed without adventure, and also without dinner. Soon after dark we arrived at the snow line on the Owyhee hills, and reached the last station. While another change of horses was being made, we obtained our supper.

Then we were informed that owing to the depth of snow, through which only a narrow trail had been broken, it was impossible for the stage to proceed any farther. The passengers would have to walk the remainder of the distance, which was "only about eight miles, over a trail on nice clean snow." There were two horses at the station which were broken to ride. These were assigned to the passengers who were officers of the government. At this announcement, the post-office inspector, Brooks, and I were quickly mounted. We finally made our way into Ruby City, where we found warmth and comfort at the leading hotel.

I remained in Ruby City several days. The sheriff, a very capable officer, and others told me that the rumor of contemplated violence upon the judge was without foundation. It was true that several gunmen had been imported from the coast cities, to garrison the improvised forts, but none of these held any ill will toward the magistrate. His decision was thought fair and upright.

At the time of my first visit to Ruby and Silver City, several quartz mills were in operation. One of them, the Minnie Moore, was producing large quantities of silver bullion. This was cast in the form, and approximately the size, of common building brick. It was customary to ship these silver bricks on the stage. Each was put in a leather bag or satchel made for the purpose, with round leather hand-holds.

The shipments being made daily, their weight did not generally overload the stage. The snow at this time, however, had blockaded the road over the Reynolds Creek summit, which was just opened for traffic on the day I started my return trip. The bullion which had accumulated at the Minnie Moore mill was sufficient load for the light stage teams without passengers. Consequently, the human freight was requested to alight at every up grade. The requests to walk up the several grades between Ruby City and the Snake River ferry were cheerfully complied with. None of these was long, and the exercise gave us an opportunity to straighten our limbs.

At Snake River hill, however, the driver stopped his team, and told the passengers that he must "unload the stage." This hill, he said, was so steep that the horses could pull only the empty coach to the summit. He further informed us that he must carry up the bullion and hand baggage; but if we were in a hurry, and would help him carry up his load, we could make Boisé City earlier. There were mutterings of ill humor, but finally all the passengers, except my prisoner, accepted the situation with an appearance of cheerfulness. We finally arrived at Boisé City without other adventure.

"My companion pointed to one of the men sitting
across the room."

CHAPTER TWENTY-EIGHT

PLAYING THE RÔLE OF A DETECTIVE

THE winter of 1865 to 1866 proved to be one of unusual
severity. Snow fell early and deep, making traffic between the mining towns and Boisé City very difficult.
Placer mining, for several months, was entirely suspended,
and the miners' cabins were so deeply buried that the occupants had to tunnel through the snow to get in and out.
During such periods of isolation, reading matter of all
kinds was at a premium. Some of the miners preserved
the copies of newspapers that they were fortunate enough
to secure during the summer, and read and reread them.
But the library of a miner's cabin usually consisted of
nothing more than a Jaynes' or Hostetter's Almanac,
and they were studiously perused. Beginning with the
signs of the zodiac, the miners read paragraph after paragraph, until they were familiar with the prescribed
treatment for tapeworms, and the many ills the human
family is likely to suffer.

It was one of these periods of isolation, one day while

Judge Kelly and I were alone in my office, that a typical
Norseman entered and asked if I "ban Mr. McConnell."
Upon being answered affirmatively, he said : "I ban told
you vas a detective ; and I ban robbed, and vould like you
to catch dat robber."

"Of what have you been robbed and where ? "   I asked
him.

He then told me that he owned a placer claim on California Gulch, not far from Placerville, and lived in a cabin
near his claim.   He said that, as there was no bank in
which he could deposit his gold dust, he had for safety
buried a Preston and Merrill yeast-powder can containing
one thousand dollars in dust, a short distance from his
cabin.   A ditch, which carried water for mining purposes,
had been constructed along the side of the hill above
where he had buried his dust, and the water had over-
flowed and washed the yeast-powder can bare.   Some person who came along that morning discovered it and carried
it away.

"When did this occur ? "   I asked.

"Last Yuly," he answered.   It was then January, fully
six months after the loss had occurred ; yet this man had
traveled through deep snow, from his claim to Idaho City
and from there to Boisé City, a total distance of about
fifty miles, hoping that I would be able to recover his treasure.   He had, from time to time, whenever he visited
Placerville, rehearsed his tale of woe to a little Irishman
named Tommy Nealy, who was a justice of the peace in
Placerville.   Owing to his official position the miner supposed the justice should be able to recover his lost gold
dust.

Finally Nealy said, "You go to McConnell, at Boisé.
He is a whale of a detective.   He will find your dust."
An American would have known that Nealy was per-

petrating a joke, but the miner being a foreigner, and having recently read a number of wonderful detective dime novels, accepted Nealy's advice in good faith, and finally found his way into my office.

After listening to his story, I asked him, "Do you know of any person's passing by that morning where you had your dust buried ? "

He said he knew of only one person, but he knew that man would not take it, for he was a friend of his.

"Where is that friend of yours now ? " I asked.

"I tank he ban in Boisé," was the reply.

Securing my hat, I started for the door, telling him to come and show the fellow to me. We made our way to a resort called a bakery, where pies and cakes and beer were sold. I knew that foreigners of almost every nationality made this resort their principal headquarters.

The room was filled so densely with tobacco smoke that at first entrance we could not distinguish faces. Seated at the many tables were groups of men, talking in various tongues. After gazing intently a few minutes through the thick atmosphere, my companion pointed to one of the men sitting across the room, and said, "Dat is my friend."

The man was watching us, and had probably recognized the man who was with me. As I crossed the room, he arose and confronted me. He proved to be a young man, probably twenty-five years old, a fine specimen of manhood. He made no resistance when I placed him under arrest. I asked him what he was doing in Boisé. He replied that he was on his way to Portland, Oregon. Then I asked him how he intended to go, and he answered that he was going on the stage to Umatilla Landing, and from there on the river boat. I searched him, and found on his person about fifty dollars in gold dust, and three dollars and fifty cents in silver. Where was the balance of his money, I demanded. He said he had no more.

That answer convinced me that he had the stolen gold dust. I knew that the stage fare from Boisé City to Umatilla Landing was forty-five dollars, and passage on the steamboat from the Landing to Portland was eighteen dollars, a total of sixty-three dollars for fare alone, besides meals at $1.25 each while on the way. He could not travel to Portland on the amount I found on his person.

My next move was to lock him in the city jail. Then, visiting the express office of Wells Fargo and Company, I found that my prisoner had not shipped out any gold dust through that channel. Upon further inquiry, I learned that he had arrived in Boisé City but a short time before I had arrested him. He had come from a place known as Williamson's ranch, on Dry Creek, on horseback, a distance of about fourteen miles. The horse he rode from the ranch was in a yard behind a harness and saddle shop on Main Street, nearly opposite the resort in which I had made the arrest.

I had asked my prisoner where I would find his baggage. He denied having any. I did not believe that was true, for nearly all foreigners retain some kind of a receptacle, brought from the "old country," in which they carry with them such relics as remind them of home and the days of their childhood. I reasoned that if my man had such a cherished relic, he would quite likely leave it near where he had left his horse.

It appeared probable that he was acquainted with the harness maker. If such was the case, his bag was likely to be left in the harness shop; and if he had such an old relic, and had the gold dust, it was likely to be in his bag with his other souvenirs. I therefore hastened to the harness shop, but found it closed and the door locked. It was by this time late in the afternoon, but too early for a business house to close. My suspicion was aroused, and I concluded to remain at the door until the owner came. I had a wait of perhaps half an hour, during which the harness maker was watching me from the resort where I had made the arrest.

At the end of that time, seeing that I was not likely to leave the front of his shop, he crossed over, and asked, "Vot do you vant?"

"I want to look through your shop," I returned. "Open the door."

Upon gaining admission, I found it too dark to make a satisfactory examination, so I asked for a light. He produced a candle. Looking around, I discovered that the owner carried a large stock of leather, in rolls thrown in confusion at one side of the shop. I could see no baggage, but the disorderly manner in which I found his stock made me suspicious. Handing the candle to the proprietor, I said, "I am not a harness maker, but I will show you how I would keep my stock if I were."

Then I proceeded to pile up his rolls of leather, after the manner of cordwood, and under the rolls of leather I found an old bag. In this I discovered the yeast-powder box with the stolen gold.

In making his complaint, the miner testified that the box he had lost contained one thousand dollars in gold dust. As Preston and Merrill yeast-powder boxes were commonly used as receptacles for dust, I knew that such boxes would hold only approximately seven hundred dollars' worth of the average quality of gold dust. I was dubious as to the value of the dust he claimed that the yeast-powder box, or can, contained. Lest there might be a shortage, for which I might be held accountable, I requested Judge Kelly to go with me and see the dust weighed.

When I opened the box to have the contents weighed, I found the gold dust soaking wet. The box had evidently been buried, and but recently dug up. Pouring it into a gold pan and placing it on the heating stove, I dried it thoroughly. Then I transferred it to the gold scales and weighed it, before the judge and other persons present. Its value at sixteen dollars an ounce proved to be a trifle more than one thousand and fifty dollars. Actually it was worth twenty dollars an ounce, or a total of more than two thousand five hundred dollars. It was as nearly pure gold as was ever mined. Further inquiry revealed that there was but one gulch, or ravine, in Idaho or surrounding territories where such pure dust was found.

The district court being in session at the time, the trial of the accused speedily followed. As the chain of evidence was complete, conviction was the result, and a sentence of three years in the territorial prison was the penalty. The Boisé City prison during those days was merely an adobe building, so obviously insecure, that to prevent the escape, it was customary to shackle the prisoners. This not only prevented escapes, but also indicated whether the accused was a hardened criminal. A man, like a horse, when hobbled the first time, finds it difficult to move around, but eventually he becomes accustomed to the shackles.

The young man convicted of taking the gold dust was so hampered by the shackles, that it was evident that he was a novice in their use. It was quite likely that his present misstep was his first offense. Owing to this, and to the fact that imprisonment for three years with hardened criminals would probably wreck his life, a petition was circulated, after he had served six months, asking the governor to pardon him. The petition having received the signature of practically all who were aware of the circumstances, including the miner whose dust he had taken, the governor granted clemency. So ended my detective story.

"A few minutes later we were placed in position, each of us determined to finish the other."

CHAPTER TWENTY–NINE

FIGHTING A DUEL

AMONG the professional men who came to Idaho City during its "boom days," was an attorney named W. W. Doughett. He brought with him the credentials of a college in Virginia, his native state, and showed the courtesy and refinement of a true Virginian. His manner of addressing the court, and his fellow attorneys, at once gave him that distinction. One year later he was followed by his sister. Report said she had been banished from the Federal lines in Virginia for carrying contraband news; hence she was known as 'the Rebel Spy."

There were two leading hotels in Idaho City at the time of Miss Doughett's arrival, the City Hotel and the Poujade House; both as highly respectable as the best hotels of today. The Poujade House was named after its proprietor, who was of French ancestry. The landlady, his wife, claimed lineage from the bogs of Ireland. Mrs. Poujade brought with her to Idaho two sisters, who assisted in the dining room and in doing the chamber work. The younger had but recently graduated from the Sisters' school at Vancouver, Washington. The elder sister, Miss Susie, was approaching that age which the irreverent call the "old maid" stage; in fact, she had "crossed the Rubicon." She was boss of the hotel, and as a consequence no foolishness was allowed. Physically she was an athlete, and morally she was a noble woman. I made the Poujade House my headquarters while in Idaho City, and retained a room there where I kept my extra clothing. Susie looked after it, and recalling those days, I realize that she looked after me, as well as my clothing. She advised me as a mother, or older sister, would have guided me.

It was at this hotel that Attorney Doughett secured room and board for his sister, "the Rebel Spy." She was soon the same as a member of the Poujade family. Being accepted on similar terms, I met her frequently in the public parlor and learned to respect her as an accomplished and estimable young lady. "Nannie," as she was called by her friends, had many admirers. Most of her friends, however, did not become suitors, owing, I presume, to her formal manner. The editor of the Democratic paper published in Idaho City was more ardent, but she did not reciprocate the tender passion, and gently but firmly rejected his proposal.

During the fall of 1866, a delegate to Congress from Idaho Territory was to be elected. As a nomination by the Democratic convention was equivalent to election, the contest prior to and pending such nominations was keen and bitter. There were, however, but two aspiring candidates, E. D. Holbrook, to succeed himself, and W. W. Doughett. For several weeks prior to the convention the Democratic editor just mentioned had advocated the nomination of Doughett. Only a few days before the convention was to meet he transferred his support to Holbrook. But few persons, at that time, knew that Doughett's sister had rejected the editor, and I am free to state that although on friendly, and somewhat confidential terms with the young lady, I did not know that he was even trying to win her hand.

The nominating convention met in due time in Riggs and Agnew's saloon, almost directly across Main Street from my office. A short time after it had assembled, I was startled by two pistol shots in rapid succession. Hastening to the street I saw a crowd of men rushing out of the saloon where the convention was being held. Crossing over, I entered at a side door and found the room redolent with the fumes of burnt powder. Mounted on a chair I saw a Boisé City attorney engaged in making a violent speech denouncing Mr. Doughett, who, it appeared, had exchanged shots with his sister's erstwhile suitor, and was then under arrest in the same room.

I took in the situation at a glance. It so happened that I had never been formally introduced to the gentleman prisoner, so I called for some one to introduce me. E. G. Sterling, Territorial Treasurer, stepped up and offered to do so. After this formality, I said to Mr. Doughett: "You appear to be in the minority here today; but you will receive fair treatment."

Turning to the speaker on the chair, Theodore Burmester, I stated: "Gentlemen, I will hold any man personally responsible who insults Mr. Doughett while he is under arrest."

Mr. Burmester got down from the chair.

I was prompted to take that stand out of friendship for Mr. Doughett's sister, and a natural desire to see fair play. Although there had never been a thought of courtship between Nannie and me, owing to the fact that I could love only one girl, yet I noticed that the editor, H. C. Street, seemed startled when I took sides in the trouble. It probably flashed upon him that I was the cause of his rejection, and subsequent events confirmed this probability.

During the previous months, I had been planning my business affairs with the purpose of visiting my boyhood home in Michigan. Having completed my arrangements, I resigned my position at Boisé soon after the convention episode. For the purpose of bidding my friends good-by, I paid what I believed was a farewell visit to Idaho City. Having said good-by to my friends, I left Idaho City early the following morning on my return to Boisé.

It chanced that the *Union*, announcing my departure, had stated that I had made some money in Idaho, and was returning to Michigan to visit my father; it also stated that I had made a good officer, and the people would be glad to welcome me back. At Boisé, I secured a ticket on the stage which was to leave for Chico, California, the following afternoon. When the hour for departure arrived, I was standing in front of the old Overland Hotel surrounded by a group of friends. Suddenly Rube Robbins, on a foaming horse, came dashing down the street and exclaimed, "Here! you cannot take that stage, you must go back and fight!" Handing me a copy of the *Idaho World* issued that morning, he said, "Read that!"

On the front page, I saw that the editor had copied from the article in the *Union* the paragraph which stated that I had been "an excellent officer" and the people would be glad to welcome me back, and added this comment: "Yes, excellent officer indeed! When he was organizing a band of cattle and horse thieves into a Vigilance Committee, for the purpose of hanging and shooting Democrats; it is a pity he is gone." The editor thought

I had departed on the stage which left Boisé one day earlier, but I had been detained one day, and consequently Rube was enabled to overtake me with the paper.

Reading the statement today, it appears incredible that it was considered sufficient cause for sending a man to bring me back, and I can offer no adequate apology for going back. I simply lacked moral courage to deny my friends, knowing as I did that they had probably already circulated the information that I would come back and call the editor to account for his slanderous article. Hill Beachy, the proprietor of the Chico stage line, was among the friends who had assembled to see me off. Turning to him I asked if he would return my fare. He readily complied with my request, and removing my baggage, which was already aboard the stage, I announced my readiness to return to Idaho City. After we were well started on our return, I told my friend Robbins that I did not intend to punish my accuser too severely. I thought a horsewhipping would serve the purpose of satisfying my friends, and prevent him from being so gay in the future.

Upon our arrival at Idaho City the following morning, we learned that Street, in anticipation of my probable return, had provided for his safety. He had engaged the attendance of two ex Confederate colonels, to act as his bodyguard. They were constantly with him. This precaution on his part prevented me from carrying out my purpose of giving him a horsewhipping. An attempt to do so would inevitably have precipitated a street fight, which would involve his friends as well as mine.

To avoid such a contingency, I concluded to send him a challenge. Accordingly, I engaged the service of a personal friend to act as my second. The challenge was accepted, and in due time articles were drawn, and signed in duplicate by both principals and seconds. It was agreed that we were to fight with duelling pistols, each party to select his own weapon. The meeting was to occur on a piece of level ground, immediately below the warm springs bathing resort. The hour set for the meeting was four o'clock A.M. It was stipulated that the meeting should be kept secret in order to avoid possible arrest. It was also stipulated that no person should be allowed on the ground except the seconds and each principal, one friend besides a surgeon and a man engaged to load the weapons.

The last stipulation was impossible to observe. That there was to be a duel had leaked out. It was customary in those days for men who carried revolvers to take them at regular intervals to a gunsmith, and have them reloaded and put in order; especially was that the custom of those who ranked as "gunmen" or killers. The gunsmith who enjoyed this patronage was a personal friend of mine, and as it happened was engaged to load the weapons at the morning meeting between Street and myself. As there was an unusual demand for reloading revolvers at a late hour the night before that meeting was to occur, he understood that the fighters were to be out in force, and passed the word out to my friends.

I had secured a room at the warm springs and stopped there the night previous to our affair. Although I had no knowledge of the fact, my friends had guards stationed around the place to protect me from possible harm. I had arranged to be called at 3 : 45 A.M. When I came out on the veranda, I discovered that we were to have at least one thousand spectators to witness our morning entertainment.

Before loading the weapons, the gunsmith, Baily Simpson, remarked that he believed that it was customary to fire a blank cartridge from each to make certain that they were clear. No objection being made, he discharged a blank from Street's pistol and found it clear, but when he had loaded mine with a similar blank and attempted to discharge it, the cap exploded, but failed to ignite the charge. Investigation revealed that a bullet had been forced into the pistol, without any powder behind it. The weapon had been cleaned and pronounced in good order the evening before, and had been in the actual possession of my second except while he left it in the buggy to go and call the surgeon, whom he had promised to bring down with him.

While the gunsmith was extracting the bullet from the pistol, Wash Underwood, a former deputy sheriff under the murdered ex-sheriff Pinkham, came to me, riding a powerful gray horse, and said: "Here, McConnell, is the best horse in the Basin. I make a present of him to you; you may want to take a ride." Pointing down the road toward Boisé City, he continued, "Avoid that point of timber and there are not men enough in this county to take you. There are three men in that timber prepared to murder you if you go down that road. We stood guard over you last night, and watched them as they made a detour above the swimming pond to keep out of sight. You will find a lunch tied behind, and two navy six-shooters at the horn of your saddle."

Up to that time, I had never intended to injure my adversary seriously. I could hit him where I wished, and I intended to deprive him of a couple of fingers from his pistol hand. But the fact that appearances indicated that my pistol had been tampered with during the temporary absence of my second, and the further fact that it was contemplated to murder me if I survived the duel and attempted to leave, aroused my deepest anger. I determined that I would show my adversary no indulgence; and if I was followed on the mountain trail that I had planned to take, I would wait for and meet my pursuers at some favorable point of rocks.

Some good angel, however, as had happened before, and often since, had evidently assumed guardianship over me. Had I been able to carry out my plan for vengeance as the circumstances appeared to justify, I would have been compelled to flee the country, and would have been marked as a renegade ever after. But that which was planned for my destruction, proved to be the cause of my salvation.

My second, when he came to realize that he had permitted unfriendly hands to gain possession of my pistol, became excited. After Baily had completed loading it, and was about to place the cap on it, he told the gunsmith to prime it. The powder used at such meetings is called English duelling powder, and is very fine. The tubes of duelling pistols are bell muzzled, and if during the process of loading any powder has entered the tube, it should be knocked out before the cap is adjusted, the explosion of the cap being sufficient to drive the flame through the fine hole at the bottom of the tube and discharge the weapon. But apparently the gunsmith, as well as my second, was excited. Under other circumstances, he would have known better, yet he followed instructions and primed the weapon. This incident, which seemed so trifling, was my salvation.

A few minutes later we were placed in position, each of us determined to finish the other. His pistol rang out clearly, but he failed to hit me ; while mine, with its primed tube, hung fire, to the extent that there were two distinct reports, the cap and tube, followed by the charge. The locks of such pistols are so stiff that unless they explode freely it is impossible to hold them on the object you desire to hit. Thus ended our bloodless duel.

I take pleasure in stating that I never believed that my opponent was a party to either of the foul attempts upon my life. Owing to my indignation, however, upon learning that his friends were involved in the effort, I undoubtedly would have held him responsible with his life, if my pistol had not failed me.

To avoid the appearance of trying to escape prosecution for engaging in a duel, I remained in Idaho City a sufficient time to give the authorities opportunity to set the wheels of justice in motion. Finding that no action looking to my punishment was contemplated, I returned to Boisé.

Before adding "finis" to this story of settling a dispute on the so-called "field of honor," I must give the sequel to the tale. Approximately twenty-four years after the duel, Idaho was admitted into the Union. While I was engaged in making campaign speeches, I arrived at the beautiful little town of Hailey, where I was met at the railroad station by a delegation of political friends, and escorted to the principal hostelry, kept by that genial host, Art Smith. He at once conducted the party into what was, in those days, the revenue-producing department of every well-conducted hotel, where I, as was expected, "set 'em up" for the crowd. After we had indulged a few times, I stepped out on the hotel porch. Noticing a tall man at the further end who had not joined the convivial party, I asked his name, and was informed that he was Judge Street. "I must speak to him," I responded.

Stepping up behind, I slapped him on the back, and exclaimed, "Hello, Judge! The last time we met, we took a shot at each other; now let us take a drink."

He cheerfully complied. During that political campaign, although he was editing a Democratic newspaper, no editor of my own political faith gave me more friendly notices than he. He had doubtless ascertained, long before, that I was not instrumental in causing him to lose that charming girl, "the Rebel Spy." She had married another, and was then a grandmother.

"Within an hour my bride and I were on our way to the Golden State."

CHAPTER THIRTY

THE DAWNING OF HAPPIER DAYS·

My plan after the duel had been, as before, to go back to my old Michigan home via California. In Bôisé, however, I learned that the Piute Indians were taking their summer outing on the warpath, in the region traversed by the Chico stage line. They had recently massacred two companies of Chinese, who were on their way to the Idaho placer mines. I concluded, therefore, as discretion is said to be "the better part of valor," that I would give the Chico route as wide a berth as possible, and go to the coast via Portland, Oregon. Accordingly I took passage on the stage for Umatilla Landing on the Columbia River.

Umatilla at that time was the point to which all supplies destined to the Boisé mines were shipped. It was termed a "wide-open town," and was all that term implied. I had learned that Aleck Stewart, one of the men who had been sentenced by the Payette Vigilance Committee to be hanged, and whom I had aided to escape, was among the wild ones there. Being desirous of meeting him, I secured the escort of a policeman to accompany me. He would most likely be found in one of the saloons, and probably some of the men whom the Vigilance Committee had encouraged to leave Idaho would be in the same resort. I did not care to enter such so-called "sporting places," so I requested my escort, the policeman, to look for him and invite him out. He did so. When Aleck came, we walked across the street and sat down upon a pile of lumber, before we exchanged a word.

Then he said, "McConnell, I am glad to see you; I never expected to see you again."

"Why?" I asked.

"Well," he answered, "you have no idea how many men have sworn to take your scalp."

"No," I replied, "I do not know the number; but assassins are all cowards, and such men have a wholesome fear of both my hands and my gun."

He then asked me how I was "fixed for money."

Thinking that he was about to ask for a loan, I replied, "I am not very well fixed. I have made some money, but it has taken a good deal to keep me."

"If you need any money, just say so," he returned. "I have money, and all I possess, even my life, is yours."

"No, Aleck, I did not come to you for money," I said. "I have looked you up to try to induce you to take yourself and your brother Charley back home to your old father and mother in Canada. The class of men with whom you and he must associate in such towns as Umatilla Landing are enough to demoralize any man. Eventually they meet violent deaths or go by the alcohol route. *Quit them while you can*," I urged, "and take Charley with you. Your hope for future happiness is with your parents, who are now old and need their boys."

The only reply he made was, "McConnell, you are right." He made no promises; but he accepted my advice.

We arose from the pile of lumber, and after shaking hands I left him there, his thoughts made tender by memories of home and mother. I have never met him since, but I shall ever cherish the recollection of that, our last meeting.

I arrived at Portland the following evening. Securing a saddle horse, I rode out to Yamhill County the next day. My intention was to spend a few days visiting among my former pupils and friends. But, as has often happened, "the best laid plans o' mice and men gang aft agley." Cupid had shot a dart at me some time before, and the arrow had penetrated more deeply than I realized.

A few weeks later I led to the altar a young lady whom I had met while I was teaching in that neighborhood. I will not attempt to describe the many charms of her who became my wife. She has been my faithful companion and helpmate up to the present time, a period of more than half a century. Our "golden wedding" day, long past now, was one filled with golden memories indeed.

All of my plans to return to my old boyhood home were suddenly changed into those for making a real home of our very own. Marriage had brought new responsibilities, delightful ones, but they must be met at once. Where should we make our home, was the question. We pondered over it and finally I resolved to go into Humboldt County, California, and establish a cattle ranch. With that purpose in view, our horses were saddled. Within an hour after we were made man and wife, my bride and I were mounted and on our "honeymoon" trip on our way to the Golden State.

The long horseback journey was by no means a trying one for my bride. Daughters of the Oregon pioneers, you must remember, were trained equestriennes. My young wife's early training had fitted her especially to be the wife of a cowboy. It was a wedding journey thrilled with happiness and hope.

The rich experiences that followed during our life together in California, and afterwards when we returned to live in Oregon and then in Idaho, would make another volume. But that is a different story from the one told in this little book. The old Vigilante days were over. The Wild West had been tamed, to a degree at least, that made it possible for the law-loving citizens to pursue in comparative safety their uplifting vocations. A new era of peace and prosperity had dawned in the great empire of the Rockies.

OX-TEAM DAYS ON THE OREGON TRAIL

By EZRA MEEKER

Revised and Edited by Howard R. Driggs

In 1852 Ezra Meeker left Iowa to make the hazardous journey by ox team to Oregon. After fifty-four years of struggle in the development of the northwest country he retraced his journey, again by ox team, in order to induce people to mark the famous Oregon Trail which the pioneers had used.

This book is the thrilling, true story of what Mr. Meeker has seen and done—of the struggle through an unknown country to win and finally to hold the West, and of efforts to preserve the memory of the Trail.

The account reflects the real spirit of Americanism, and will go far to humanize our history through its vivid pictures of the brave men and women who helped push our frontier to the Pacific.

Cloth. x + 225 pages. Illustrated. Price $1.20

WORLD BOOK COMPANY

YONKERS-ON-HUDSON, NEW YORK
2126 PRAIRIE AVENUE, CHICAGO

THE WHITE INDIAN BOY

By E. N. Wilson

In collaboration with Howard R. Driggs

EVERYONE who knew "Uncle Nick" Wilson was always begging him to tell about pioneer days in the Northwest. When "Uncle Nick" was eight years old, the Wilson family crossed the plains by ox team. When he was only twelve, he slipped away from home to travel north with a band of Shoshones with whom he wandered about for two years, sharing all the experiences of Indian life. Later, after he had returned home, he was a pony express rider, he drove a stage on the Overland route, and he acted as guide in an expedition against the Gosiute Indians.

"Uncle Nick" knew pioneer life and he knew the heart of the Indian. So Mr. Driggs persuaded him to write his recollections and helped him to make his story into a book that is a true record of pioneering and of Indian life with its hardships and adventures.

The White Indian Boy is an exciting, true story that has interested many boys and girls and contributed to their understanding of the early history of the West.

Cloth. xii + 222 pages. Illustrated. Price $1.20

WORLD BOOK COMPANY

YONKERS-ON-HUDSON, NEW YORK
2126 PRAIRIE AVENUE, CHICAGO

IN THE NORTH WOODS
OF MAINE

By E. E. Thomas

FIFTY years ago, before lumbering operations became extensive in northern New England, essentially the same conditions were to be encountered as in the Colonial times. Therefore, this story of two boys who spent the winter of 1875 trapping and shooting in the wilds of Maine is an authentic, first-hand picture of experiences similar to those of the pioneers. As such it provides an account of one phase of the settlement and expansion of our country.

The two boys lived almost wholly on their own resources; their experiences were varied and exciting. The story of that winter is filled with adventures that will give boys and girls of today a clearer conception of the hardships faced by the early settlers, who had the added danger of Indians. In addition to being a reflection of pioneer life, this little book is an interesting account of the woods and the wild life in them.

The illustrations are attractive line drawings made by an artist who is noted for his accuracy in portraying animals. The appendix contains brief descriptions and sketches of some of the more important northern animals.

Cloth. viii + 109 pages. Illustrated. Price 88 cents

WORLD BOOK COMPANY
YONKERS-ON-HUDSON, NEW YORK
2126 PRAIRIE AVENUE, CHICAGO

DEADWOOD GOLD

A STORY OF THE BLACK HILLS

By George W. Stokes

In collaboration with Howard R. Driggs

THE life and work of the pioneer miners who opened up the golden treasures of the Black Hills form a stirring chapter in the history of the winning of the West. The story as told in this book is a vivid one, made more valuable and interesting because Colonel Stokes writes of his own experiences. He was one of the first to reach the new gold diggings in the seventies, and he saw the whole development from the early exciting days, on during the mad rush to Deadwood, to the discovery of some of the greatest gold mines in the world.

There is in this volume much historical and geographical information. Especially does the book give a realistic picture of many aspects of the gold mining process and of the activities associated with the great gold rushes of all times. Serving as a supplementary reader in intermediate grades, this true story of American adventure will hold the interest of boys and girls.

Cloth. xii + 163 pages. Illustrated. Price $1.00

WORLD BOOK COMPANY

Yonkers-on-Hudson, New York
2126 Prairie Avenue, Chicago

PIONEER LIFE SERIES

HIDDEN HEROES OF THE ROCKIES

By Isaac K. Russell
In collaboration with Howard R. Driggs

A collection of true and thrilling stories gathered together from the diaries, memoirs, and letters of pioneers, that gives briefly, but vividly, the history of the blazing of the trail across America's last frontier.

In the great desert basin lying between the Rocky Mountains and the Sierras, were enacted some of the most daring and epoch-making adventures in our history. Until a few years ago little was known of the struggles and hardships encountered by the early explorers who first penetrated into the Great Salt Lake region and charted the great American desert. Hidden Heroes of the Rockies gives the first connected account of these pre-pioneers. It brings to light new names of heroes that have remained hidden for more than a century.

Although intended primarily as a supplementary reader in the intermediate grades, the book will interest mature readers as well as boys and girls.

Cloth. xii + 295 pages. Illustrated. Price $1.36

WORLD BOOK COMPANY

Yonkers-on-Hudson, New York
2126 Prairie Avenue, Chicago

BREAKING SOD ON THE PRAIRIES

BY CLARENCE W. TABER

A STORY of early days in Dakota when the settlers, following in the wake of the soldiers, first planted their homes on the plains. It presents a realistic picture of the pioneering of our northern prairie lands and of the bitter struggle to transform the vast stretch of new country into the productive and habitable states of today.

The characters of the story were real persons and the events related are true. The author tells about his own rich experiences during those beginning days, when the settler, no less hardy and courageous than the pathfinder who had preceded him, was confronted with new problems connected with subduing the soil.

This book is not alone a convincing story; it gives many lessons in the nature and geography of what has become our great wheat belt, and in recording the true story of one boy it exemplifies the part which many young Americans took in the development of our country.

Cloth. viii + 292 pages. Illustrated. Price $1.36

WORLD BOOK COMPANY
YONKERS-ON-HUDSON, NEW YORK
2126 PRAIRIE AVENUE, CHICAGO